RECONSTRUCTION

RECONSTRUCTION

A Tragic Era?

Edited by SETH M. SCHEINER

Rutgers University

ROBERT E. KRIEGER PUBLISHING COMPANY
MALABAR, FLORIDA

Cover Illustration:
The New Orleans Massacre. The freedmen's march to the
Mechanics' Institute and the struggle for the flag. (From
Harper's Weekly, August 25, 1866; New York Public Library)

Original Edition 1968
Reprint Edition 1978

Printed and Published by
ROBERT E. KRIEGER PUBLISHING COMPANY, INC.
KRIEGER DRIVE
MALABAR, FLORIDA 32950

Copyright ©1968 by
HOLT, RINEHART AND WINSTON, INC.
Reprinted by arrangement

Printed in the United States of America.

Library of Congress Cataloging in Publication Data

Scheiner, Seth M.,   comp.
    Reconstruction, a tragic era?

    Reprint of the ed. published by Holt, Rinehart, and
Winston, New York, in series: American problem studies.
    Includes bibliographical references.
    1. Reconstruction—Addresses, essays, lectures. I. Title.
[E668.S36 1978]   973.8   78-12422
ISBN 0-88275-748-2

10   9   8   7   6   5   4

CONTENTS

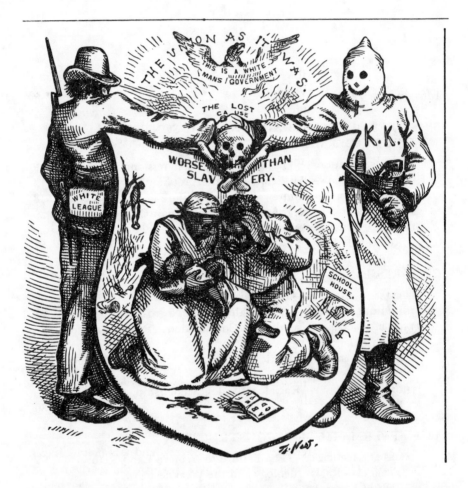

The Plight of the Freed Negro. Cartoon by Thomas Nast. (From *Harper's Weekly*, October 24, 1874; New York Public Library)

INTRODUCTION

After four years of Civil War, the victorious North faced the problem of reconstructing the Union. While the North's victory signified the defeat of the southern interpretation of states' rights as manifested in secession and nullification as well as the imminent end of slavery, it did not resolve the dual issue of readmitting the defeated states and the future status of the freedmen. During Reconstruction the nation divided on just what course of action should be followed. Were the Confederate states to be treated as conquered provinces or errant members of the family? Or had they committed "state suicide" or forfeited their rights? Were Negroes to be accorded rights equal to those of whites, and what assistance should they receive in their transition from slaves to freedmen?

After heated controversy, Congress enacted legislation in an attempt to arrive at a solution to these questions. The Civil Rights Act accorded Negroes legal rights on the same basis as whites, the Freedmen's Bureau Act provided assistance for them in the exercise of these rights and their adjustment to freedom, and the Reconstruction acts (1867) established the process by which the southern states would be readmitted to the Union. Scholars have inquired into the wisdom of these laws and the motivations behind them. Their investigations center around the question: Was Reconstruction a "tragic era"?

Historians have generally divided Reconstruction into three periods, but they have disagreed on the wisdom of the proposals, the motives of individuals, the tactics employed, and the effect of policies pursued in each phase. The first phase deals with the disagreement between Congress and Abraham Lincoln, and then Andrew Johnson, over the procedure by which the southern states should be reconstructed. Congressional opposition to Lincoln's plan for the speedy and lenient readmission of the southern states marked the opening of the struggle over who should take the lead in reconstructing the South. After the assassination of Lincoln, the legislative-executive battle continued during the administration of Andrew Johnson. Congress emerged from the conflict victorious. It passed over Johnson's veto the Civil Rights Bill, the Freedmen's

1

Bureau Bill, and the Reconstruction bills, which placed the southern states under military rule until they adopted constitutions acceptable to Congress.

Scholars have raised important questions concerning the controversy between the President and Congress: Was the congressional program the handiwork of a small coterie of self-seeking and vindictive individuals within the Republican party, or did it express the commitment of a majority of that party to the principle of civil equality for the freedmen? Was the program enacted by Congress inferior to the Lincoln-Johnson plan? If the congressional plan was an unwise one, what degree of responsibility for its passage must Andrew Johnson bear?

Reconstruction entered its second phase with the passage of the Reconstruction acts in 1867. Congress now put its program into operation. Southern governments established under Congressional Reconstruction—called Radical because of the alleged relation of these governments to the Radical Republicans—varied in duration from three years in two states to ten years in three. Students of the period have examined such issues as the extent and importance of corruption and high taxes, the aims and abilities of government officials, the nature and quality of the new constitutions, and the role of the Negro as a voter and public official. The reader will note that some of the following selections stress excess and misrule, while others emphasize the complex nature of Congressional Reconstruction.

While the final period—from 1877 until about the turn of the twentieth century—falls outside of the limits of Reconstruction, it is crucially related to any discussion of the era. What transpired in the aftermath of Reconstruction is a measure of the success or failure of the era itself. The alleged weaknesses of the Reconstruction settlement are often held responsible for the collapse of the Republican party in the southern states and the Negro's decline in status after President Rutherford B. Hayes removed the last of the troops from the South—the so-called Compromise of 1877. This section of the book returns us to the basic question: Was Reconstruction a tragic era?

The debate on the first phase, congressional versus presidential Reconstruction, opens with a selection by James Ford Rhodes. Writing early in the twentieth century when most Americans wished to eradicate all manifestations of sectionalism, Rhodes defended Lincoln's plan for the speedy restoration of the Union. But Lincoln's program fell victim to the blunders of Andrew Johnson. Through political errors and intemperate statements that alienated moderate elements, Johnson made it possible for a small group of vindictive, tyrannical, and misguided Radicals led by Thaddeus Stevens and Charles Sumner to force through a reluctant Congress an injudicious Reconstruction program. Rhodes believes that the nation could have avoided the tragedy of Radical Reconstruction if Johnson had provided enlightened leadership.

Rhodes's view prevailed until the late 1920s and early 1930s, when a new group of historians took issue with his characterization of Johnson and his analysis of Radical motivation. Influenced by an economic interpretation of history, they looked beyond a desire for revenge to explain Radical motivation. As a spokesman for this point of view, Howard K. Beale presents Johnson in a more favorable light and shifts the primary responsibility for failure of the Lincoln plan to the shoulders of the Radical Republicans. He attempts to show that Johnson was the victim of a coalition of Radical congressmen and northern industrialists and financiers intent on advancing their own economic interests. This Radical-business alliance feared that passage of the Johnson program for a speedy return of the South would permit that section to join forces with the agrarian West in repealing the pro-business legislation adopted during the Civil War. What strategy, according to Beale, did the Radicals and their business supporters devise to prevent such an outcome and thereby advance their selfish interests?

Since World War II many historians have reconsidered the economic interpretation of the conflict between Congress and the President. They have raised serious questions on the approach to motivation. For these historians, Beale attributes to the opponents of Johnson a unity that did not exist. Beale along with Rhodes not only fails to give appropriate emphasis to the Republican commitment in behalf of civil equality for the freedmen but omits reference to the Johnson camp's anti-Negro prejudice and political aims.

Beale's defense of Johnson as a victim of Radical treachery comes under strong attack from Eric L. McKitrick. To a large extent, McKitrick's study parallels that of Rhodes in its condemnation of Johnson's leadership and its assumption that the Lincoln plan was superior to that advanced by the Radicals. Like Rhodes, he insists that when Johnson assumed office he had the opportunity to obtain the backing of the moderate majority in Congress but he lost its support. The inability of Johnson to provide effective leadership can be traced to his lack of self-assurance, his inflexibility, and his tendency to view politics in personal rather than party terms. It is on Johnson's failure as a party leader that McKitrick centers his study.

In his discussion of both the Freedmen's Bureau and the Civil Rights bills, McKitrick expands upon Johnson's failure to work with the moderate leadership. Johnson never used his power as President and his influence as party leader to consult, to bargain, and to compromise with congressional leaders. Instead he piled mistake upon mistake, so that in the end even the vast majority of moderate Republicans were compelled to desert him. On this point, the reader will find McKitrick's analysis of the experience of a leading moderate, Lyman Trumbull, particularly illuminating.

While McKitrick re-evaluates Beale's view of Johnson as a political leader,

Stanley Coben takes issue with his economic interpretation of the presidential-legislative conflict. After re-examining the statements and proposals of the Radicals and northeastern businessmen, he concludes that while economics may have influenced the behavior of many of these men, they were not united on "any specific set of economic aims." Contrary to Beale's assertion that these two groups presented a united front on the tariff and currency issues, Coben emphasizes divisions within the business community which precluded such an alliance. Does the Coben selection, then, cast doubt on the validity of an economic interpretation as the explanation of Radical motivation? In attempting to answer this question, the student should consider the selection by LaWanda and John Cox.

The Coxes second the thesis of Rhodes and McKitrick that Johnson's actions alienated the majority of Congress, but unlike Rhodes and Beale they see more to the struggle between the legislative and executive branches than either presidential bungling, or Radical vindictiveness and despotism, or an economic alliance between certain northern interests. They believe that the contest must be "viewed in the context" not only of a Democratic desire to reorganize the parties to advance its own political interest, but also of the Johnsonian opposition to, and the overwhelming Republican fidelity to, civil equality for the freedmen. The Coxes show that while anti-Negro attitudes permeated the Johnson camp, Republican thought had moved from mere opposition to the extension of slavery into the territories to a definite commitment in favor of equal civil rights. By 1866 most northerners had come to consider the call for legal equality moderate rather than radical. In the end, civil rights emerged as "the issue of Reconstruction."

In the Coxes' view, Johnson's supporters used the term radical for political purposes and with little concern as to whether it really applied to their opponents. They doubt if the congressional desire for a share in formulating a Reconstruction program can be considered radical. Their study suggests that Beale, Rhodes, and contemporary critics of the congressional plan confuse the real issue when they equate the positions of Stevens and Sumner with the aims of all Republican opponents of Johnson. Unity was something the Republican opposition lacked except in its determination to prevent readmission of the South until it accorded the freedmen legal equality. Does the Coxes' argument suggest a challenge to the underlying assumption of Rhodes, Beale, and McKitrick that Radical policy was unwise? The answer becomes crucial in understanding the role of Johnson in the clash between the Radicals and the President.

Following passage of the Reconstruction acts in 1867, Congress proceeded to implement its program in the South. On this phase of Reconstruction, too, historians have disagreed. William A. Dunning, in the next selection, advances the traditional view that Radical rule foisted upon the South a decade of malignant rule.

Dunning began his study of Reconstruction at about the same time that Rhodes was writing his history of the United States. In addition to his own writings, he trained and influenced numerous graduate students who produced Reconstruction studies of individual southern states. The Dunning school, as the master and his disciples came to be known, maintains that a coalition of ignorant ex-slaves, venal carpetbaggers, and reprobate scalawags inflicted upon the South an era of maladministration which brought it to the verge of ruination. Radical rule was marked by fraudulent elections, preferential legislation for the freedmen, innumerable episodes of corruption, and the highest taxes in the history of the South. The social philosophy at the end of the nineteenth century with its emphasis on white supremacy accounts, at least in part, for Dunning's castigation of Negroes possessing only limited training and ability, men who had no race pride, casting votes in state legislatures and at polling places throughout the South. In the end, southerners reacted to Congressional Reconstruction by looking forward to the day when the licentious Radical governments would be driven from power.

Except for an occasional dissenter, the Dunning view went unchallenged until the 1930s. As belief in the superiority of the white race affected the interpretations of Rhodes and Dunning, so did the increasing adherence to racial equality in the thirties bring about a climate of opinion that was to leave its impact on historiography. The arguments must be reviewed with this in mind. In their studies, revisionist historians have stressed the complexities of Reconstruction. For them, the era was marked by many enlightened measures, not merely by high taxes or corruption. Their findings have led the revisionists to contest the Dunningite characterization of Reconstruction as a tragic era.

A passage from John Hope Franklin's *Reconstruction After the Civil War* presents a challenge to Dunning's description of Negro participation in Reconstruction. Synthesizing the findings of some three decades of revisionist scholarship, Franklin advances the thesis that the Negro leaders—who were in the main educated, capable, and diligent—attempted no social revolution or vendetta against former slaveholders. How different were they in ability, character, and conduct from the average public official? While granting that most of the freedmen lacked the preparation "to participate effectively in a democracy," he points out that their qualifications differed little from those of the mass of whites added to the voting rolls during the Jacksonian era. The extension of the franchise to the freedmen must be studied in the context of the American commitment to the principle of universal manhood suffrage.

Revisionist scholars also have brought into question the Dunningite representation of Radical rule as retrogressive. In the next selection, Jack B. Scroggs offers evidence that disputes studies which restrict themselves to describing only the corruption and high taxes of the carpetbagger governments. Our view of Reconstruction has been substantially modified by his focusing attention on the carpetbagger conventions that added many progressive features to the state constitutions—greater protection for the debtor, more liberal voting and officeholding requirements, improvements in the area of education, and more equitable taxation and apportionment systems. Those states in which the carpetbaggers had the greatest influence produced the most progressive and democratic constitutions. Scroggs as well as other revisionists, then, considers the results of Congressional Reconstruction far more complex than the Dunning school's monolithic description of the period as a tragic era.

In *The Era of Reconstruction*, Kenneth M. Stampp expands upon the revisionist contention that Reconstruction defies a simplistic explanation. By looking at the era from this point of view, he submits that the Radicals cannot be placed into a single category; they must be studied in the broader context of southern as well as national history. The carpetbaggers and scalawags were not a pack of scoundrels but an assemblage of groups with divergent motives and varied abilities.

Along similar lines, he is critical of the superficial manner in which the Dunning school presents the corruption, the increased governmental costs, and the high taxes of Radical rule. He concedes that dishonesty plagued the Reconstruction governments, but he notes that it was also a phenomenon of Republican and Democratic rule on the national, state, and local levels. Corruption permeated the short-lived state governments established by Johnson in 1865 and the administrations that drove the Radical regimes from power. Nor did the Radicals use all of the increased taxes to line their pockets. They directed a substantial portion to rebuilding the South, improving its transportation facilities, and providing public services for Negroes as well as .hites. In short, Stampp inquires, were the Radical governments condemned for their alleged radicalism and corruption, or for attempting to turn the freedmen into political supporters?

Up to this point, the selections concerned with Congressional Reconstruction fall into two schools: the Dunning and revisionist. But Thomas J. Pressly adds another dimension to the debate when he brings into the discussion the problem of the historian's ideological convictions influencing his findings. Whereas Dunning wrote at a point in American history when the theory of Negro inferiority was widely accepted, Stampp has formulated his conclusions in an age that has substituted for this theory the concept of racial equality. Pressly is disturbed that at some future date another historian writing under the influence of the ideology of his day will repudiate Stampp as Stampp has rejected Dunning. To guard against this pitfall, he urges historians to make use of quantitative techniques—applying the methodology of statistics to historical data—as a supplement to traditional approaches. Advocates of this method believe that by using quantification historians will be influenced less by their own ideology and can then base their interpretations on more durable evidence.

The final section of this book examines the aftermath of Reconstruction, in particular the Negro's decline in status following the Compromise of 1877. Two scholars writing in the revisionist tradition, James M. McPherson and W. R. Brock, explore the extent to which Reconstruction legislation met the basic problems faced by the freedmen. McPherson attempts to show that Radical Reconstruction failed to accord Negroes the economic security necessary to make legal equality meaningful. Many of the abolitionists who were still active during Reconstruction believed that the freedmen could improve their position only if they received land. Accordingly, they urged Congress to go beyond civil rights laws and redistribute the land of rebellious southerners to the freedmen. Despite abolitionist appeals and a few philanthropic enterprises, the federal government rejected these proposals. Left landless and economically insecure when Reconstruction came to an end, Negroes were vulnerable to violations of their legal rights. For McPherson, this rather than the alleged excesses is the great tragedy of Reconstruction. His examination of the shortcomings of the era is put into the broader framework of ideology by W. R. Brock.

In concentrating on the ideology of Reconstruction, Brock develops the argument that Radical adherence to racial equality ran counter to the experience and science that buttressed mid-nineteenth-century racial ideology. Since the vast majority of white northerners and southerners did not accept racial equality, the rights granted the Negro were erected on an insecure foundation. The wording of the Fifteenth Amendment left the Negro's right to vote subject to the capriciousness of the dominant group. Why does Brock argue that the distinction between universal and impartial suffrage as well as rights and privileges weakened the Negro's position?

The nature of nineteenth-century racial ideology leads Brock to conclude that the freedmen required positive government aids not extended to whites. Congress refused to provide such assistance. Radical Reconstruction operated within a nineteenth-century bourgeois liberalism that rejected government intervention. Thus, when Radical enthusiasm for racial equality faded, there were no institutional bulwarks to protect the freedmen from a white majority who considered Negroes their inferiors.

The ideology of racial inequality no doubt affected the relations between whites and Negroes in the individual states. Joel Williamson and C. Vann

Woodward, in concluding the debate, direct their comments to the emergence of segregation in the South and its relation to Reconstruction. Williamson in his study of South Carolina presents evidence that a definite pattern of segregation emerged from the everyday practices of race relations. The desire of whites to protect their racial purity, and therefore preserve their superior civilization, led to the separation of the races. Under a system of segregation, southern whites discovered that they could keep the Negro in a subordinate position. But contrary to the Dunning school, which held that the excesses of Reconstruction led the white South to reduce the status of Negroes to that of second-class citizens, Williamson finds segregation to have been a fact before southern whites regained political power. C. Vann Woodward in *The Strange Career of Jim Crow* joins Williamson in rebutting the Dunningite rationale for the emergence of segregation, but disagrees with his assertion that segregation became an established part of southern life during Reconstruction.

While Woodward grants that there were incidents of segregation during Reconstruction, he warns that it would be an error to equate the pattern of race relations in this period with either the ante-bellum years or the Jim Crow system of the early twentieth century. Too many "cross currents and contradictions" barred the development of a comprehensive pattern of segregation by the close of Reconstruction. Woodward finds that for approximately two decades after the Compromise of 1877 segregation practices lacked the rigidity and uniformity which were to be essential characteristics of race relations in the twentieth century. This period was an era of experimentation and uncertainty in race relations; it was an age that offered alternatives to the Jim Crow system. According to Woodward, the South decided in favor of a comprehensive pattern of segregation only after this transitional period—and not until Reconstruction had long passed.

Was Reconstruction, then, a tragic era? Did it cause a breakdown of the democratic process in the South? Was the social and economic development of the South retarded? In the long run, did Radical Reconstruction hurt the Negro more than it helped him? The answers to these questions are important for an understanding of Reconstruction as well as the years that followed. For the era had long-lasting effects upon the relations between white and black, North and South, President and Congress. Indeed, the debate as to whether Reconstruction was a tragedy is still very much with us.

[In the reprinted selections footnotes appearing in the original sources have in general been omitted unless they contribute to the argument or better understanding of the selection.]

JAMES FORD RHODES (1848–1927) turned to history after a successful career in the coal and iron industry. Even though he attended college for only two years and was never formally trained as a historian, his seven-volume *History of the United States from the Compromise of 1850* (1893–1906) led to his election as president of the American Historical Association. In 1919 and 1922 Rhodes added two volumes that carried the story through the administration of Theodore Roosevelt. Historians have generally commended his coverage of political and military aspects, while pointing out serious limitations in his treatment of the social and economic. In an extract from this work reprinted here, Rhodes expresses preference for the Lincoln plan. However, he considers the Radical Republicans divisive and Andrew Johnson incompetent.*

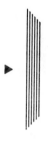

Presidential and Congressional Failure

. . . When Andrew Johnson became President he endeavored to reconstruct the shattered Union substantially on the lines which Lincoln had laid down. He imposed three conditions on the late Confederate States which they must comply with before they should be entitled to representation in Congress. These were, the repeal of their ordinances of Secession, the abolition of slavery by their conventions and the ratification of the Thirteenth Amendment by their legislatures, and the entire repudiation of their State debts incurred in the prosecution of the War. These conditions were with slight exceptions complied with and, on the assembling of Congress in December 1865, it seemed to Johnson that the senators and representatives elect from the Southern States ought to be admitted to their seats in the Senate and the House. It was evident, however, from the beginning that Congress proposed to have a hand in this important work and through a Joint Committee on Reconstruction and the Committees on the Judiciary they constructed a policy of their own imposing still other conditions on the Southern States. They passed a law conferring full civil rights on the negro and widened the scope of the Freedman's Bureau

* From James Ford Rhodes, *History of the United States from the Compromise of 1850* (7 vols.; New York: The Macmillan Company, 1906), vol. VI, pp. 1–47, *passim*. Footnotes omitted.

which had been established before the death of Lincoln. They adopted the Fourteenth Amendment and required of the Southern States its ratification before they should be restored to their old place in the Union. President Johnson vetoed the first Freedman's Bureau bill, February 19, 1866 and somewhat later the Civil Rights bill, and thereby became involved in a quarrel with Congress which was intensified by vituperative speeches of his and of Thaddeus Stevens, the leader of the House of Representatives. When Congress adjourned in July 1866 the executive and legislative departments of the nation were at swords' points and both appealed to the country for endorsement. An exciting campaign followed. Johnson lost his chance of securing a third of the House of Representatives by his foolish and disgraceful stumping tour through the country and the victory of the Republicans was overwhelming, a majority being secured of considerably more than two-thirds of the next Congress. . . .

Although President Johnson was thoroughly discredited at the North, such was the importance and power of his office that he was still able to render the South and the whole nation a valuable service if he could bring his mind to the acceptance of the country's verdict. If he recommended to the Southern States the ratification of the Fourteenth Amendment, they would undoubtedly take his advice and this would be the basis of reconstruction. . . . [H]e was in a position to do this without any sacrifice of principle. It would undoubtedly require a sacrifice of individual opinion, of self-love, but upon this depended an important advantage to the nation. The

popular will had been unmistakably manifested in the elections—and it was the will of the party which had chosen him—and if Johnson could not lend himself to the execution of that mandate he ought to resign. But he was inexorable and his message to Congress of December 3, 1866, was only a rehash of his old ideas, though with a sauce less peppery. Evidently he had learned nothing. The Northern people were weary of his iterated complaint that the Southern States remained unrepresented; by now, indeed, they gave but small heed to anything he said. In the South he had a real influence but this he would not exert in the right direction. During the previous session of Congress he had lost whatever reputation he had possessed for statesmanship. . . .

On the first day of the session after the holidays [January 3, 1867] Stevens called up his bill to provide for valid governments in the ten States on the basis of negro suffrage and white disfranchisement. This was a substitute for the bill of the Joint Committee on Reconstruction, reported at the previous session, which offered in set terms the Fourteenth Amendment to the Southern States as the sole further condition of their restoration to their former rights and privileges, and it engaged the attention of the House for several weeks. Bingham speaking for a number of Conservatives made a plea that Congress stand by the Fourteenth Amendment and give the Southern States more time for its consideration. "There is something grander in magnanimity and mercy," he said, "than there is in stern, relentless, even-handed justice." It might have been expected that these noble words would sway Congress. The North could afford to be generous. The Fourteenth Amendment plan had been worked out by an able committee after long deliberation and with great care and it bore the marks of constructive genius. Congress adopted it, the people by an overwhelming voice had approved it. The Southern States it is true had refused to accept it but they were misguided and the knowledge of who had misguided them was in the possession of Congress. . . .

Despite the irritation caused by the rejection of the Amendment by the Southern States such were the differences which cropped out when the details of any measure were considered, that no further act of reconstruction would probably have been passed at this session had it not been for the able and despotic parliamentary leadership of Stevens. The old man's energy was astonishing. Vindictiveness seemed to animate his frame. Already bitter enough in his personal antagonism to Johnson and the Southern people he added to this bitterness by frequent consultations with those whom he termed "loyal men from the South" who hated "the natural leaders of opinion" the men of "brain experience and education" in their section and who aimed at supplanting them in political influence and power.

The original bill and Stevens's substitute were recommitted to the Joint Committee on Reconstruction which was composed of the same senators and representatives as at the last session. During two meetings the committee considered the subject and agreed, with the consent of all the Republicans but one, on a bill which Stevens was ordered to report to the House. This he did on

February 6. The bill set aside "the pretended State governments" in the ten late so-called Confederate States and placed them under military rule, dividing them into five military districts over each of which the General of the Army [Grant] should place a commandant. The commandant should preserve peace and maintain order. He might use the legal tribunals if he found them competent but they were to be considered of no validity *per se*. The reason for this proposed legislation was given by Stevens the day after his introduction of the bill. "For two years," he said, the Southern States "have been in a state of anarchy; for two years the loyal people of those ten States have endured all the horrors of the worst anarchy of any country. Persecution, exile and murder have been the order of the day within all these Territories so far as loyal men were concerned, whether white or black, and more especially if they happened to be black. We have seen the best men, those who stood by the flag of the Union, driven from their homes and compelled to live on the cold charity of a cold North. We have seen their loyal men flitting about everywhere, through your cities, around your doors, melancholy, depressed, haggard, like the ghosts of the unburied dead on this side of the river Styx, and yet we have borne it with exemplary patience." . . .

Bingham opposed the bill unless it could be improved; other Republicans objected to it and argued in favor of delay. John A. Griswold, an enterprising manufacturer and liberal business man from Troy, New York, preferred to stand by the Fourteenth Amendment, to wait for "the development of events" rather than to take "a step in the wrong direction" and to give "those States further opportunity to exhibit a spirit of obedience and loyalty." Griswold's remarks were made on February 8, the day on which the vote was expected. Stevens called for the previous question and in his endeavor to carry the House taunted those who opposed his bill with having been convinced by the arguments of the President. But the House refused to second the previous question and the debate went on.

Among others, Bingham and Blaine offered each an amendment to the bill but Stevens would not allow them to be voted on; finally these two were fused into one which added a section to Stevens's bill providing a termination to the military rule by the reconstruction of the late Confederate States with universal suffrage, the negroes having the right to vote, and there being no disfranchisement practically of the whites. Blaine moved that the bill be referred to the Committee on the Judiciary with instructions to report it back immediately with the Bingham-Blaine amendment. This motion was voted down. . . . Before this vote was taken Stevens apparently sure of success made the closing speech. I have no respect for the Fourteenth Amendment, he declared. He vented the whole power of his sarcasm on Bingham; he called the Bingham-Blaine Amendment a "proposed step toward universal amnesty and universal Andy-Johnsonism"; it "lets in a vast number of rebels and shuts out nobody." He intimated that the ex-Confederates were "great criminals" whose crimes were "unrepented" and seemed also to imply that they were "vagabonds and thieves." The Republican members who urged mercy were "hugging and caressing those whose hands are red and whose garments are dripping with the blood of our and their murdered kindred." He demanded the previous question and his bill passed without amendment. . . .

Stevens carried this bill through an unwilling House; a strong minority of his own party was opposed to it largely for the reason that pure military rule without any provision for its termination was unpalatable. He obtained his majority by sarcasm, taunts, dragooning and by cracking the party whip. . . .

While the Reconstruction Acts were not as "thorough" as Stevens and Sumner desired, they are nevertheless the heroes of this legislation: without them it would not have been enacted by the Thirty-ninth Congress and possibly not at all. Stevens, who may be said to have inspired the military control and the disfranchisement provisions, was without constructive genius but he had the power of carrying measures devised by other men through the House by overbearing all opposition. . . .

Most revolutions go too far and so did ours, but it undoubtedly would not have done so had not Lincoln been killed. Three men are responsible for the Congressional policy of reconstruction: Andrew Johnson by his obstinacy and bad behavior; Thaddeus Stevens by his vindictiveness and parliamentary tyranny; Charles Sumner by his pertinacity in a misguided humanitarianism. Emerson's words tell the story, "They mix the fire of the moral sentiment with personal and party heats, with measureless exaggerations and the blindness that prefers some darling measure to justice. and truth."

A professor of history at the universities of North Carolina and Wisconsin for more than two decades, HOWARD K. BEALE (1899–1959) advanced an economic interpretation of Reconstruction which historians have labeled the Beale thesis. Historians have acclaimed not only his examination of Reconstruction but also his investigations of subjects ranging from American education to the foreign policy of Theodore Roosevelt. In his study of the election of 1866, *The Critical Year: A Study of Andrew Johnson and Reconstruction*, Beale dissents from Rhodes's condemnation of Johnson. He attributes the misfortunes of Reconstruction to an alliance of Radical Republicans and northern businessmen desirous of securing political hegemony over the agrarian South and West. The reader should take particular note of Beale's discussion of "claptrap and issues."*

An Economic Interpretation

In any campaign the issues which the politicians raise and questions which actually interest the public are apt to be confused. In 1866 they were inextricably entangled. Postwar excitement, dormant bitterness, and fear provided the Radicals with excellent raw material for a campaign of hysteria; hence most political speeches were largely claptrap. For the issues one must seek further. Important issues there were. But most of them were avoided because the Radicals regarded them as dangerous to their cause, and the Conservatives thought it futile to push them until the states were all back in the Union. On some questions opinion was hopelessly divided in both Radical and Conservative camps. The Radical campaign was waged to keep in power the party that had carried on the War and was still in the saddle in 1866. Conservatives sought to restore the Union in order to end the Radical monopoly of power and throw the government open to free competition of interests and sections, realizing full well that a return of the South would greatly improve their own chances of controlling the government. To these respective ends the leaders worked. Ultimate

* From *The Critical Year: A Study of Andrew Johnson and Reconstruction* by Howard K. Beale, copyright, 1930, by Harcourt, Brace & World, Inc.; copyright, 1958, by Howard K. Beale. Reprinted without footnotes by permission of the publisher. Pp. 139, 141–148.

victory would depend upon the ebb and flow of a neutral popular opinion.

. . . Most historians and thoughtful public men now condemn the Radical program of reconstruction. Yet it was adopted. These men differ in analyzing the causes underlying the failure of the Johnson policy, but they generally agree in assigning as chief among them the unreasonable conduct of the South and the stubbornness and stupidity of Johnson. While they condemn the man, many have come to regard Johnson's policy as the most statesmanlike of any. Some of his bitterest enemies lived to acknowledge this. Yet it failed. To understand its failure and Radical success, comparative wisdom of policies and constitutional theories must be thrown aside as inconsequential; other factors popularly thought to be determining issues must be reduced to their true 1866 proportions, and the methods and spirit of the campaign must be studied. Reconstruction was decided not through a consideration of the wisdom of various plans, but by a skilful use of the tools of political campaigning.

The Radicals for one reason or another feared the return of Southerners to participation in government. After a great war, bitterness was natural. Men who had lost loved ones in battle, did not look with pleasure upon the return to power of the men who had slain them. Allowed to cool and tempered by a return of friendly commercial and political intercourse, this sentiment would soon have subsided, for magnanimity to a vanquished foe is not difficult. In the West and in the border communities, numerous relationships had bound North and South before the War; between these sections passions had fired more quickly, and conflict had raged more violently than between the South and more distant New England. But after all, reconciliation was easier between two interrelated sections which knew each other's good qualities, than between the South and a remote Northeast which condemned each other as inherently wicked, and hated each other with the hate of long years of abolition controversy.

While resentment against Copperheads was most violent in the West and border East, bitterness toward the South was cooling rapidly in non-abolitionist circles and, let alone, would gradually have died out. Abolitionists, however, had embraced as part of their creed belief in Southern wickedness, expressed in their definition of the Constitution as "a covenant with death and an agreement with hell." Many New England teachers and preachers throughout the North continued with all sincerity to paint Southerners as disciples of the devil. Those who held this view of the South, opposed its return to participation in government.

To many, abolitionism had become a religion which made it a God-given duty, now that the slaves were free, to elevate them to civil and political equality with the white man. Many such "Niggerheads" knew nothing of the Southern negro, but they devoutly believed in their own theories; others of them actually worked with the negroes as missionaries and teachers, but like many reformers were blinded to practical difficulties by their own enthusiasm. Typical of these sincere "friends of the negro" was Charles Sumner.

Men did actually believe that if the "rebels" were allowed to regain political power, they would yet overturn the government. Many feared the return of "traitors" to offices from which loyal men would be displaced. But often such expressions of fear merely signified that a man dreaded to see good Republicans replaced by Democrats.

Many Northerners honestly saw in the Black Codes a Southern attempt to re-enslave the black; others were interested in the negro chiefly because his vote would be a Republican one, and would counteract that of his white neighbor.

But a considerable group dreaded the return of Southerners to power not because they feared disaster to the nation, but because they foresaw in it injury to themselves, their section, or their class. For many years Southern statesmen had controlled the destinies of the country. Since the days when her own young-bloods had urged secession for New England, the industrial Northeast had been a "minority section." It was not power-less on questions where South and West divided, or where factors which bisected every community were concerned, but on such issues as the tariff or an agricultural or industrial dispute New England and the increasingly industrial Northeast were still a minority section. For thirty years Southerners or Northern "Doughfaces" had been supreme in the federal government. Now after a long and bloody war, a purely Northern party had conquered the South and won for itself and its section long-sought power which was not lightly to be surrendered. Sheer love of power made many men hesitate before voluntarily relinquishing it by allowing Southerners to return to Congress. To politicians, whose chief function is to elect themselves and members of their party to office, retention of

control seemed a sufficient cause for Radicalism, but this motive could not be publicly avowed.

For years before the War, the Northeast had been unable to get protection for industry. Then during the Civil War high taxes on industry had made necessary a high tariff, and, with the South out of the way and the North rather evenly divided, protectionists had managed to make the tariffs more than cover the taxes they supposedly offset. If the South were readmitted before this high tariff was permanently established, the protectionists would be overwhelmed.

Bondholders throughout the country feared, and were encouraged to fear, a repudiation of the debt through a return of Southern representatives. The South was traditionally opposed to national banks; hence, Eastern bankers and supporters of the new national banking system dreaded to see the South return. Hard money men, deflationists, business men who wished federal protection in the extension of their business into what they feared would be an inhospitable South, land speculators who sought confiscated lands, and new corporations that feared government regulation or sought government aid, shared this dread. The growing capital-owning group of the Northeast, then, sought to keep the South out until through negro suffrage it could be brought under Northern control. The agricultural and debtor classes, on the other hand, would have welcomed Southern aid in Washington. Here was really in a new phase the familiar American struggle of East against West, old settled region against frontier, business against agriculture, city against country, "haves" against "have-nots," that made a civil war of the American Revolution, that turned Jeffersonians against Hamiltonians, Jacksonian Democrats against Whigs, and more recently farm bloc against Wall Street. This old antagonism and not a difference of opinion on the condition of Southerners, was what divided Conservatives and Radicals in 1866.

Radical leaders faced a perplexing problem. They were only a minority group. The two major issues motivating their campaign were their stand on various economic questions and their desire to secure the Republican Party in power. But the Radical leaders could not ask the people to support them merely because of their desire for power. Still less did they dare raise the economic questions. Indeed, they had to fight desperately against their being raised by the Conservatives, for on economic issues they would have lost half their party.

On the reconstruction issue unconfused, the major portion of the people originally supported Johnson; hence, the Radicals had to raise mere shibboleths. Had other Radicals been as fair-minded, as public-spirited, and as tolerant as Governor Andrew, Johnson's reputation would not have been destroyed, and there would have been no split between Congress and the President. Andrew, though a negro suffragist, deprecated the Radical tactics. "I am opposed to public meetings," he said, "called in support of . . . any man, leader or party. . . . Now, if one set of men get up meetings for Paul, another set will get up meetings for Apollos. The result will be antagonism, not patriotism; and intensifying, and exaggerating the importance and value, of the relatively unimportant, chance-utterances of individuals in con-

troversial moods; which ought if possible, to be forgotten. . . . I, for one, desire not to encourage popular excitement, most of all, not to aid in making any." But in the creation of this very situation which Andrew deplored, lay the Radicals' best hope of success.

The repudiation shibboleth was safe throughout the country. In the East economic issues could be insinuated into the campaign, for Eastern supporters knew well the stand Radical leaders would take on them; in the West, when the Conservatives raised them, they were shouted down as nonpolitical and irrelevant. Talk of the return of rebels to power conveyed a plain second meaning to the protectionist and to the creditor, whereas it was taken at face value in the West. If the South could be excluded, or admitted only with negro suffrage, the new industrial order which the Northeast was developing, would be safe. Intentionally, then, the issues were befogged. Definite economic questions of importance confronted the country, issues on which a majority, even without the South, would have supported Johnson against the Radicals, issues which ten years later arose to plague the country. In 1866 these questions were pushed into the background, the South was kept out, and the Northeast succeeded in establishing minority government until the new industrial forces were strongly enough entrenched to withstand attacks.

Throughout the campaign constitutional arguments bulked large. It was a day when constitutional theories were required for all practice. But in our Anglo-Saxon world constitutional theories are derived from practice, not practice from theory. People were vitally interested in deciding whether the South should have its former place in the government or should be held in subjugation for a period of years, but they were not much interested in the theory of the right or wrong of either course, except as a justification in law for what they intended to do in practice. Lawyers and Congressmen, true to form, made lengthy speeches on matters of constitutionality, for this gave them an air of erudition, and satisfied the legalistic conscience of their constituents. Nevertheless constitutional discussions of the rights of the negro, the status of Southern states, the legal position of ex-rebels, and the powers of Congress and president determined nothing. They were pure shams.

We have already found that the condition and temper of the South, especially in the light of biased fabrication or deceptive half-knowledge, proved a favorite topic of political oratory in 1866. In a study of the issues this and the negro question and the Fourteenth Amendment must not be accepted at their campaign valuation. Other factors not recognized in the campaign literature as issues, must be considered because of their potential and actual importance. Politicians' tricks and machinery must be studied as the really determining factor. Claptrap and issues must be distinguished.

The role of party leader is an important function of the presidential office. President Andrew Johnson's failure to exert leadership in dealing with Congress is the subject of the following selection from *Andrew Johnson and Reconstruction* by ERIC L. McKITRICK (b. 1919) of Columbia University. By emphasizing Johnson's relations with the moderates in Congress, he takes direct issue with Beale's interpretation. While McKitrick's views to a large extent follow those of Rhodes, there is an important difference in emphasis. The reader may also profit from a comparison of McKitrick's discussion with the selection by LaWanda and John Cox.*

Andrew Johnson's Failure as a Party Leader

The historian's reappraisal of the Johnson administration has been a reaction both against the personal indignities suffered by President Johnson and against the character of reconstruction as it was eventually inaugurated by Johnson's congressional opponents along lines differing so vastly from those advocated by the President. It is natural to connect the one with the other—and it is thus rather hard to avoid the conclusion that of the two policies it was Johnson's which contained the greatest long-range wisdom and which best seemed to serve the interests of the country at large.

Still, the question remains: what came in between? What was there about the speed and completeness of Johnson's collapse that renders such a version of "wisdom" almost beside the point? There must have been, in Johnson's policy and in the manner in which it was promoted, a challenge so basic and so widely felt that considerations of morality, wisdom, or the "interests of the country" temporarily lost a great deal of their ordinary meaning.

Here it will be necessary to summarize briefly the leading facts, so that they may later serve as points of reference.

* Reprinted from *Andrew Johnson and Reconstruction* by Eric L. McKitrick by permission of The University of Chicago Press. Copyright © 1963 by The University of Chicago. Pp. 6–12, 310–318. Footnotes omitted.

By May, 1865, Andrew Johnson had decided that the initial problems of re-construction—of re-establishing civil governments in the rebellious states and preparing those states to resume their normal functions in the Union—might best be handled, not by calling a special session of Congress, but by a continued exercise of executive powers. His first major step was taken on May 29. On that day he issued two proclamations, one of which laid down the terms whereby individual Southerners at large might obtain amnesty. This was done under the authority of the President's pardoning power. In the other, which he issued in his capacity as commander-in-chief of the armed forces, he ap-pointed a provisional governor for North Carolina and authorized him to establish a government there, thus set-ting postwar reconstruction on its way. He was shortly to issue similar proclama-tions for six other states. Lincoln him-self had acted by proclamation at moments when he preferred, at least temporarily, not to be hampered by the more cumbersome process of acting jointly with Congress. Here was a prob-lem sufficiently analogous to those which Lincoln had faced, together with a pre-cedent sufficiently recent, that Johnson's step did not at the time seem unwar-ranted. Although the country was no longer in a state of war and although there were some doubts as to the appro-priateness of launching so deeply im-portant a project as reconstruction except by closely united executive-legis-lative procedure, generally speaking there was at first very little serious ob-jection to the President's action. His was simply the opening step, not neces-sarily challenging any basic principle. It was generally supposed that his purposes

and those of Congress would prove, in due course, to have been more or less in harmony throughout.

Indeed, the proclamations in them-selves were not such as to afford undue grounds for misgiving. The amnesty policy, in addition to its general provi-sions, contained qualifications which guaranteed, at least in principle, that large categories of former participants in the rebellion would come under in-dividual scrutiny before being granted full pardon. Nor did the other proclama-tion—the one for North Carolina, which was to serve there and elsewhere as the basis for presidential reconstruction—foreclose the possibility of reasonable guarantees and safeguards for the future loyalty of any state governments that might be set up in the South. Federal agencies were re-established there, and the provisional governor was directed to appoint civil officers, state and local, giving preference to loyal people. A constitutional convention was to be called which would amend the state's organic law in conformity with the re-sults of the late conflict. Properly con-strued, this implied a warning that cer-tain conditions would have to be met before such states and their reconstructed governments could be considered for full recognition by federal authority. Presumably the Executive would make these conditions clear and explicit by private correspondence. The provision most open to question was the one di-recting that the convention—or the legislature that would later be elected—should prescribe the state's qualifications for voting and officeholding. Consider-able sentiment existed in the North favoring suffrage, in some qualified form, for the newly freed Negroes; and thus the wide individual discretion which this part of the proclamation allowed to a former slave state may not have been the most effective way of promoting such an aim. And yet here, too, the possibility of informal pressure remained theoretically open. Only the radical extremists of the Republican (or Union) party showed immediate signs of alarm.

There is a sense in which it could be said that "reconstruction" proceeded with remarkable smoothness during the summer, fall, and early winter of 1865. Numerous observers, taking note of Southern conditions immediately after the collapse of the Confederacy, commented upon the widespread sense of shock, amounting virtually to apathy, exhibited by the people of that region. With little notion of what to expect from the conqueror, the majority of the population was immersed in the dull awareness of defeat. It was thus hardly an extravagance to report that they "accepted the situation"; nothing could be more unanimous than this very point, in dozens of such reports; and to add, as General Grant did in his, that it was "in good faith," was almost a *non sequitur*: it scarcely mattered. Submission to force was complete and beyond question; no tendency to further rebellion could be discerned anywhere; and the most dominant and definite of political desires—insofar as they existed at all—was the desire for speedy reunion. The functions of local government were resumed, and delegates to conventions were chosen, mainly without incident.

After the conventions had done their work—voiding the prewar ordinances of secession, abolishing slavery, and repudiating the rebel state debt—regular elections were held in the course of

which were chosen state governors, state legislatures, and members of Congress. By late fall these legislatures had been organized and were in session. When a legislature had ratified the Thirteenth Amendment, the President would as a rule retire the state's provisional governor, and the elected governor would assume the full exercise of his duties. At this point—although Federal garrisons would not immediately be withdrawn—the former rebel states were, so far as the President was concerned, in full and legitimate operation. It was thus that by the end of 1865 all these states, with the exception of Texas, had been "reconstructed" and were, in Johnson's opinion, entitled once more to full rights of representation in the federal Congress.

There was, however, another sense in which the process had been anything but satisfactory. Once it had become certain that the Southerners were not to suffer wide-scale reprisals and that summary punishment was not to fall upon their leaders, another kind of uncertainty had apparently been allowed to invade their minds; they were not precisely sure what was now expected of them. There was a margin of doubt wide enough that they were encouraged to experiment with the spirit of the requirements. A sense of decision in complying with these requirements was lacking in all the conventions; the irritable Northern observer was struck by a legalistic tendency of delegates to quibble, to split hairs, and to indulge themselves in the luxury of hedging. Some states would not nullify secession, but "repealed" it; others would not abolish slavery straight out, but for the record's sake simply acknowledged, in effect, its destruction by force of arms. Two of them—Mississippi and South Carolina—failed altogether to repudiate their Confederate debt before adjourning, which evoked agitated messages of remonstrance from the President. Mississippi actually refused to ratify the Thirteenth Amendment.

There had been other annoyances. The provisional governor of South Carolina had made a speech in July in which he had said, among other things, that Lincoln's death had not been the calamity for the South that many had imagined—a statement which produced a very unfortunate impression. In August, Mississippi's provisional governor, scarcely four months after the close of hostilities, had begun organizing local militias, on the grounds that they were necessary for the preservation of law and order. Although the federal commander in the state had immediately ordered a stop to all such activity, his orders were countermanded by Johnson himself; Johnson, in his anxiety to avoid friction between his provisional governor and his military commander, had discriminated between them in such a way as to anger and humiliate the latter and had permitted initiatives and prerogatives to the former which a Northern public could not yet view without hostility and suspicion. It was thus that the South—perhaps in spite of itself—was contributing, item by item, to a malaise which threatened to undermine the North's initial disposition to support, experimentally, presidential reconstruction.

By early winter two sets of developments had progressed enough to provide the North with a major focus for bitterness. One involved Southern intentions toward the masses of newly freed Negroes; the other had to do with the character of the men being elected to public office in the Southern states. Legislation defining the rights of "persons of color" was already under way in several of these states, and the "black code" of Mississippi had been substantially completed. Though the Mississippi code guaranteed certain basic civil rights (to sue and be sued, to make contracts, and to acquire property), the severe restrictions which it placed upon landownership, labor arrangements, and testimony in the courts, together with its rigorous definitions of vagrancy, were widely denounced as a savage effort to fling the Negro back into that very state of slavery from which he had so recently been lifted. Similar codes in South Carolina and Louisiana would evoke similar anger, and those of other states would seem less severe only by contrast. The right to vote, even on the most limited terms, had of course everywhere been placed quite out of the question. It is true that most of the high ideals of wartime had centered upon the sanctity of the Union, and those, on the other hand, which had to do with emancipation—and with the consequences which might follow from it—had always remained in vaguer form. Yet those ideals, such as they were, now appeared suspended in the limbo of unreality. Men who had felt them with passion now saw themselves cheated of even a token fulfilment; others who had shared them but nominally still saw them, or thought they saw them, flaunted contemptuously by a people who had temporarily forfeited any right to a hand in the settlement of such grave matters.

As for political rights in Congress, the

Southern people apparently supposed that they were now entitled without qualification to all that they had once enjoyed. Their presumptions seemed all too clearly written in the records of the men they sent to represent them. Waiting to be seated, as the Thirty-ninth Congress assembled in December, were an inordinate number of Confederate military officers and former members of the Confederate Congress. Here was a bizarre dramatization of the serious difficulties now obstructing the speedy reconciliation which had been so widely assumed, earlier in the year, to be both possible and desirable.

It was in Congress during the preliminaries to the opening of business in December, 1865, that the Northern reaction was given its first sharp expression. After the Clerk of the House, by prearrangement, had omitted from his roll call the names of the Southern members-elect, extremists of the Republican party immediately assumed the leadership in forming a Joint Committee of Fifteen to pass on the qualifications of the new claimants. Thaddeus Stevens, its most energetic member, made it clear that his committee intended to make the most extensive and unhurried deliberations, not only upon membership, but also upon the entire question of reconstruction and the adequacy of the President's policy. The implications of that policy, in short, were already thought to be sufficiently grave as to call for a minute reappraisal, down to the very fundamentals. Meanwhile, the ex-Confederate states would be kept waiting indefinitely for readmission.

Concurrently, legislation was prepared for the purpose of insuring a firmer degree of federal political control in the South and for strengthening the position of the masses of colored freedmen. The first of such measures was the Freedmen's Bureau Bill, originating in the Senate under the sponsorship of Lyman Trumbull of Illinois. By its terms the Freedmen's Bureau—the federal agency most directly concerned with the affairs of displaced Negroes —was to have its jurisdiction widened, its powers strengthened, and its life extended. Another, the Civil Rights Bill, was an even more direct response to the "black codes"; it forbade discrimination between citizens on grounds of race or color and represented an effort to assert jurisdiction for the federal government over matters which, owing to the looseness of presidential policy, had been improperly allowed to pass by default to the recently rebellious states.

It was mainly in connection with this legislation that any possibility of compromise was finally withdrawn. The President himself removed all remaining doubts by making the break open and explicit. Senator Trumbull, a man of moderate preferences and in Lincoln's time a consistent supporter of the administration, had tried to design both bills in such a way as to provide some common ground tolerable to both the President and the radicals; he had read the bills to Johnson and assumed that the President had found them acceptable. His chagrin, therefore, was considerable when on February 19 Johnson without warning vetoed the Freedmen's Bureau Bill, saying that he could not reconcile its provisions "with the words of the Constitution." Three days later Johnson, in a passionate and semi-impromptu speech, told his audience of the indignities he had suffered at the hands of the radicals, naming and denouncing those who he thought were planning to wreck his policy. The speech was generally regarded in the press as intemperate. Then, on March 27, he vetoed the Civil Rights Bill, also on the ground of doubtful constitutionality, and it was at this point that the President was abandoned by most of the Northern journals which had hitherto supported his policy. . . .

While Johnson was making up his mind whether to sign the Civil Rights Bill, examining the alternatives and weighing the consequences, he was able to draw upon the widest range of opinion to assist him in coming to his decision. Naturally he could not be expected to pay much attention to those men who, like Stevens and Sumner, were by now his avowed enemies. He need hearken only to his well-wishers, who were still numerous. [William Pitt] Fessenden, [James W.] Grimes, and [John] Sherman had all indicated their version of a basis (if one did remain) for unity. [Oliver P.] Morton had made his position clear. Trumbull had been rebuffed once; everything for him would now depend on the fate of his other bill. The President was not in the dark about where any of these men stood.

There were many others, hoping for the success of his administration, who urged their views upon him. Henry Ward Beecher wrote, "The passage of this bill will in a great degree frustrate the influence of those who have sought to produce the impression that you had proven untrue to the cause of liberty and loyalty." Governor Jacob D. Cox of Ohio, who, like Beecher, had already got into trouble for too warmly supporting the President, urged the latter that "if you can find it in accordance with your sense of duty to sign the bill, it will with our Western people make you fully master of the situation, and remove the possibility of any such opposition in the Union ranks on other measures as would prove at all embarrassing to your administration." Cox added, somewhat diffidently: "For similar reasons I believe it would assist us greatly in holding together our State organizations. . . ." Such circumspect journals as the *Nation* and *Harper's Weekly* praised the bill and did not suppose the President would see any objections to approving it. The New York *Herald* also thought it a wise measure. Republicans of temperate views, that is, took it for granted that the President's course was so clear that he himself would not fail to perceive it. Senator [William M.] Stewart of Nevada, after supporting the Freedmen's Bureau veto, was certain that Johnson would not issue another such paper. Rutherford B. Hayes wrote to his uncle: "He now seems to feel that he was misled and is really anxious to conciliate. If he signs . . . , the chances are that a complete rupture will be avoided. Otherwise, otherwise." James Garfield had also predicted that the bill would be signed. To that, one of his local lieutenants replied, "I hope so. . . . Well: we will wait and see. If he vetoes it, you have no alternative but to . . . give him the hot end of the poker."

Every member of the cabinet, except Welles, hoped that Johnson would see his way clear to signing the bill. Of the three secretaries most strongly attached to Johnson and his policy (Welles, Seward, and McCulloch), two of them turned over documents to the Executive which should have been of some assistance in determining the state of popular opinion. Thurlow Weed had informed Seward on March 6 of strong radical sentiment in New York, saying that the radicals would carry the people "if any serious mistakes are committed." A California correspondent of Hugh McCulloch told how he had tried in vain among Sacramento Unionists to moderate anti-Johnson feeling after the Freedmen's Bureau veto and the Washington's Birthday speech, even though prior sentiment had been very favorable. On the other hand, Gideon Welles, whose papers contain a remarkably full picture of political affairs in Connecticut, does not seem himself to have grasped very accurately the meaning of what his correspondents told him, and thus could not have communicated much of that picture to the President. In Welles's diary and letters one sees a mind strikingly similar to Johnson's own. Welles, who of all Johnson's advisers was the one most fiercely committed to the President's policies, actually anticipated most of Johnson's decisions simply by virtue of having already come to similar ones himself. Moreover, like Johnson, he had the habit of dismissing most evidence of opposition as the fruit of malignant radical intrigues. He so interpreted much of the political news that he got from home. But Calvin Day, one of Welles's regular correspondents, finally told him in a burst of exasperation:

It seems to me to be mere bosh to say that this Congress are tools in the hands of Stevens, Sumner, of any other ten or twenty men in Congress, & such charges whether put forth in the babbling at the White House, or in the Editorials of the New York Times or Hartford Times or C are simply childish, and are put forth simply on the principle of crying "Mad dog." I have too much respect for the office held by Mr Johnson to say he is only a tool in the hands of Weed, Blair, or Raymond, but it appears to me quite evident that for some cause he has changed his opinions & conduct & associations strangely since he left Nashville. I have never seen more *unity* or *decision* of feeling in the ranks of the Great Union party on any subject that exists to day, that the course of the President on reconstruction is hasty, unwise, & if carried out will be of lasting & incalculable injury to the country. . . .

Amid the flood of advice and counsel being received by the President at this time and upon which he might draw prior to taking action on the Civil Rights Bill, the only sector of opinion that really indicated clear, unequivocal, and virtually unanimous approval for everything he had done, and was likely to do, lay in the Democratic party. Fernando Wood assured Johnson that the New York Peace Democracy was "well disposed," and Jeremiah Black told him that his Freedmen's Bureau veto had "made millions of good hearts glad and grateful." The Pennsylvania Democracy, the President was informed by R. H. Kern, "will endorse your veto and Reconstruction policy." Likewise the Illinois Democracy ("with extraordinary enthusiasm"), according to Representative Samuel S. Marshall; the President's loyal Democratic followers in that state asked only that he withdraw a little of his patronage from disloyal Republicans and give it to them. Edwards Pierrepont of New York declared with brutal candor, "The leading men and the great body of the Republican party are not with you and they never will be," and in effect gave Johnson a Democratic version of the same advice that Oliver P. Morton would give him from the Republican side—that "all roads out of the Republican party led into the Democratic party." Pierrepont intimated that an excellent bridge between them would be the appointment of a Democrat as Collector at the Custom House.

Another letter, dated March 6, 1866, eventually made its way to the President's desk, though perhaps not soon enough to influence him much one way or the other on the Civil Rights Bill, for it had had to come all the way from San Antonio, Texas. From a delegate to the Texas constitutional convention, it assured Johnson ingratiatingly that the only men there who opposed him and supported Stevens and Sumner were those who had opposed secession—"What was called Union men." "But I can repeat what I said to you in Washington, that there is not a secessionist in the state of Texas who is opposed to you or your policy." . . .

When the President was finally ready to act, he had presumably arrived at his decision in full knowledge of all the alternatives. The spirit of that decision was perhaps best reflected in a scene which took place about this time between the President and his private secretary, Colonel Moore. The two were in the President's chamber one evening, the latter pacing the floor in deep thought. Suddenly Johnson stopped and, fixing his eye upon Moore, declared: "Sir, I am right. I know I am right, and I am damned if I do not adhere to it." It was in some such intrepid spirit that

he prepared to cut John Sherman's tightrope.

Johnson delivered his veto of the Civil Rights Bill on March 27. He said in his message that if it were necessary to declare Negroes citizens it would not be "sound policy" to take such a step with eleven of the states concerned still unrepresented in Congress. The conferring of such citizenship, moreover, would discriminate in the Negro's favor against worthy foreigners, who had to wait five years before themselves becoming citizens; it might be better for the ex-slave, "unfamiliar with our institutions and our laws," to "pass through a certain probation." The President felt that the bill would enact "a perfect equality of the white and colored races," imposing federal law on a subject wherein it had "frequently been thought expedient to discriminate between the two races." When the act presumed to punish instances of civil rights being infringed under the color of local law, ordinance, or custom, it invaded the immunities of legislators, judges, and peace officers. Putting all such cases under the jurisdiction of federal courts showed that the bill's actual intention was to strike at state judges who, acting on their responsibility and conscience, gave decisions contrary to it. Such a judge was thus a judge no longer, but "a mere ministerial officer, bound to decide according to the will of Congress." The President thought that if any one of the rights enumerated in the first section of the bill happened to be denied in any state, the federal courts then could and would take away all state jurisdiction in all civil or criminal cases involving Ne-

groes. The machinery which was speci-
fied for carrying out the bill's provisions
(the powers of arrest conferred on commissioners of the Freedmen's Bureau,
the setting-up of courts in more than one
part of a district when needed, and so
on) implied "a permanent military force
. . . to be always at hand, . . . whose only
business is to be the enforcement of this
measure." The bill was not only "fraught
with evil" in its details, but in its general
scope and purpose it exceeded all constitutional bounds:

In all our history, in all our experience as
a people living under Federal and State law,
no such system as that contemplated by the
details of this bill has ever before been proposed or adopted. They establish for the
security of the colored race safeguards which
go infinitely beyond any that the General
Government has ever provided for the white
race. In fact, the distinction of race and
color is by the bill made to operate in favor
of the colored and against the white race.
They interfere with the municipal legislation of the States, with the relations existing
exclusively between a State and its citizens,
or between inhabitants of the same State—
an absorption and assumption of power by
the General Government which, if acqui-
esced in, must sap and destroy our federa-
tive system of limited powers and break
down the barriers which preserve the rights
of the States.

It was thus that the key leaders of the
Republican party who had worked for
compromise over the past sixteen weeks
saw their last ground cut out from under
them. Fessenden and Grimes had no
more to say. It was virtually impossible
for the influential Republican journals
that had labored for conciliation to continue their support of the President after
this point. John Sherman, whose efforts
in that direction had failed and whose

predictions of harmony had proved base-
less, now found his own position (and
that of his fellow Ohioan, Governor
Cox) decidedly exposed. Sherman's mon-
itor in the legislature, the sage Warner
Bateman, sent him the word on March
30:

Diversity of opinion is rapidly disappear-
ing. . . . It is not now so much a difference
. . . as to whether we will or will not support Johnson but as to how we shall deprive
his evident defection of its power of mischief. His abandonment of his professed
purpose to protect the freedmen is conceded by everybody around except Mr. Cox
and Baber. . . . I do not doubt Mr. Cox's
entire uprightness but his superserviceable
zeal in behalf of Johnson and his policy has
I fear fatally compromised his influence with
his party. . . . I have lost faith entirely in
the President. He intends in my judgment
to betray us. . . . I cannot but regard his
vetoes as an escape from all his promises of
protection to the freedmen on the hypo-
critical pretence of constitutional objections.
His last message hands the Freedman over
helplessly to the tender mercies of state
legislation and his exasperated master. So
we go.

Lyman Trumbull made his case, and
that of the Republican party, in the
Senate on April 4. After a long analysis
of Johnson's objections (during which
he icily observed "that the President's
facts are as bad as his law"), Trumbull
recited with damning precision the
course of his own efforts to come to
terms with the President. This part of
Trumbull's speech constitutes an important source document for one of the
most unusual cases of alienation in our
political history, a case almost without
parallel in the effectiveness with which
Executive and Legislative departments
were to become for a time sealed off

from each other. It is especially significant coming from one of the few Republican senators who would later vote
against a general and concerted effort to
throw Johnson out of office.

Congress, in the passage of the bill under
consideration, sought no controversy with
the President. So far from it, the bill was
proposed with a view to carry out what were
supposed to be the views of the President,
and was submitted to him before its introduction into the Senate. I am not about to
relate private declarations of the President,
but it is right that the American people
should know that the controversy which
exists between him and Congress in reference to this measure is of his own seeking.
Soon after Congress met it became apparent
that there was a difference of opinion between the President and some members of
Congress in regard to the condition of the
rebellious States, and the rights to be secured
to freedmen.
. . . All were anxious however, for a reorganization of the rebellious States and
their admission to full participation in the
Federal Government as soon as these relations could be restored with safety to all
concerned. Feeling the importance of har-
monious action between the different departments of the Government, and an
anxious desire to sustain the President, for
whom I had always entertained the highest
respect, I had frequent interviews with him
during the early part of the session. Without mentioning anything said by him, I may
with propriety state that, acting from the
considerations I have stated, and believing
that the passage of a law by Congress, securing equality in civil rights when denied by
State authorities to freedmen and all other
inhabitants of the United States, would do
much to relieve anxiety in the North, to in-
duce the southern States to secure these
rights by their own action, and thereby
remove many of the obstacles to an early
reconstruction, I prepared the bill substan-

tially as it is now returned with the President's objections. After the bill was introduced and printed a copy was furnished
him, and at a subsequent period, when it
was reported that he was hesitating about
signing the Freedmen's Bureau bill, he was
informed of the condition of the civil rights
bill then pending in the House, and a hope
expressed that if he had objections to any of
its provisions he would make them known
to his friends, that they might be remedied,
if not destructive of the measure; that there
was believed to be no disposition on the
part of Congress, and certainly none on my
part, to have bills presented to him which
he could not approve. He never indicated to
me, nor, so far as I know, to any of its
friends, the least objection to any of the
provisions of the bill till after its passage. . . .
And yet this is the bill now returned with
the President's objections, and such objections! What are they? That—
"In all our history, in all our experience
as a people, living under Federal and State
laws, no such system as that contemplated by
the details of this bill has ever before been
proposed or adopted."

It has been assumed by most writers,
following the lead of Gideon Welles,
that such misunderstandings as those
experienced by Fessenden, Grimes, Sherman, Trumbull, and others were trace-
able to Johnson's habit of listening
politely and then making his own decisions. Such an assumption is doubtless
essentially correct. With routine callers,
that very habit has been the traditional
(indeed the only possible) refuge of
President after President. But senators
who are the leaders of the President's
own party constitute a very different
sort of case. Senators are not normally
routine callers petitioning for favors.
Nor do they customarily present themselves for the purpose of providing the

President with information upon which
he may or may not act; they know that
he has other and more systematic ways of
obtaining facts. They have come for the
transaction of government business.
They are there for the planning of
policy, for determining those areas
within which joint action is possible, and
for developing the necessary strategy
whereby such action may be effected.
Such a process is essentially one of
negotiation, whose minimum requirement is that the principals must at least
understand one another; that process,
re-enacted over and over, has underlain
the history of every successful administration known to the American party
system. So it was with the calls made by
Republican senators upon President
Johnson at various times during the
winter of 1865–1866; they were made for

the purpose of inviting negotiations out
of which, it was assumed, a successful
line of policy might issue. What Fessenden and Trumbull and the others could
not have known, however, for all their
experience and lore, was that Andrew
Johnson at no time actually assumed
negotiations to be going on. The President apparently never understood that
he was expected to bargain with leading
senators at all.

At last virtually all of them came to
realize that policy would have to be
made from this point on without the
anchor post customarily provided by the
Executive office. Indeed, the effectiveness of political discourse in the ensuing
election campaign would depend upon
the very thoroughness with which the
Republicans as a party had cut themselves loose from that post.

The following essay is one of many published since World War II that disputes the economic interpretation of the congressional-presidential controversy. STANLEY COBEN (b. 1929), who teaches at the University of California, Los Angeles, and is particularly interested in United States economic history, rejects the economic thesis as unreflective of the broad spectrum of Radical Republican and northeastern business sentiment. For him, economics alone fails to explain the actions of the Radicals and their business supporters. This selection offers the student a challenge to Beale's assertion that there was an alliance between both groups, and an important transition to the passage by LaWanda and John Cox that follows.*

The Economic Interpretation Challenged

Historians have generally accepted the view that Radical Reconstruction "was a successful attempt by northeastern business, acting through the Republican party, to control the national government for its own economic ends: notably, the protective tariff, the national banks, [and] a 'sound' currency."[1] The Radical program is also said to have been "the method by which the 'Masters of Capital' . . . expected to exploit the resources of the southern states" behind federal protection.[2] Western hostility to these eastern business designs was avoided by large appropriations for rivers, harbors, railroads, free land, and pensions, and by use of the ever-potent "bloody shirt." Thus is supposed to have been prevented a union of western and southern agrarian opposition to the industrial and financial masters of the East.[3]

This thesis has met with little serious challenge and has been subjected to only occasional qualification. It continues to influence studies of the political and economic history of the post-Civil War era.[4] Yet a closer examination of the important economic legislation and congressional battles of the period, and of

* Reprinted from Stanley Coben, "Northeastern Business and Radical Reconstruction: A Reexamination," *Mississippi Valley Historical Review*, XLVI (June, 1959), 67–78, 89–90. Most footnotes omitted.

the attitudes of businessmen and influential business groups, reveals serious divisions on economic issues among Radical legislators and northeastern businessmen alike. Certainly neither business leaders nor Radicals were united in support of any specific set of economic aims. Considerable evidence also suggests that the divisions among businessmen often cut across sectional as well as industrial lines. Furthermore, evidence indicates that few northeastern business groups were interested in southern investments in the early postwar years, and that these few were hostile to Radical Reconstruction.

The evident need for new interpretations of the motivation of northern Radicals and of the economic history of the entire period is demonstrated by a re-examination of the most important of the "economic ends" usually agreed upon as motives for Radical Reconstruction: the tariff and the currency issues, and the charge that northern business interests sought federal protection for the exploitation of the South.

The tariff split northeastern businessmen more than any other issue. So fierce was business competition in this era, and so eager were the antagonists to use every possible means of winning an advantage, that almost all important tariff schedules became battlegrounds between industries, as well as between firms within the same industry. The copper, iron, linseed, and woolen textile industries, for example, were bitterly divided on crucial tariff schedules. The most significant split, however, was between certain highly protectionist Pennsylvania interests on one side and influential low-tariff groups in New England and New York on the other. Pennsyl-

vania coal mine operators feared the competition of rich Nova Scotia deposits, mined by low-wage labor, close to major American markets. Iron and steel manufacturers, the largest highly protected interest, were faced with the competition of long-established, technologically advanced English producers, whose wage scale was only a fraction of that of the Americans. Pennsylvania carpet, glass, and wool industries demanded protection for similar reasons. The Keystone State was the largest extractor of iron ore and coal, the largest manufacturer of every form of iron and steel, of carpets, glass, and chemicals. On the other hand, powerful opposition to the tariff objectives of the Pennsylvanians came from the cotton and many of the woolen textile manufacturers of New England, and from the intertwined importing, financial, and railroad interests of New York.

New Englanders had become strong advocates of lower tariffs in the 1850's. The sharp tariff reductions of 1857 were accomplished chiefly by southern and New England votes. New England manufacturers, especially textile producers, desired cheap imported raw materials in order to lower the price of their finished goods on the international market. Furthermore, they agreed to reduced rates on manufactured goods to discourage the growth of domestic competition. Among American manufacturers, New England producers as a group were farthest from domestic sources of raw materials, closest to sources of cheap foreign commodities. Cheap supplies of coal, lumber, flaxseed, building stone, fine wool, and other commodities were available in nearby Canada and Nova Scotia. Scottish and British iron, Indian linseed, and Russian and Philippine hemp were imported into Boston in large quantities for the benefit of manufacturers. Hardly any wool for the finer grades of cloth was produced in America, either before or after the war; nor were the rough, lowest grades, used in carpets and blankets, available at home. By the end of the war, northeastern cotton manufacturers were importing the cheap Indian Surat cotton already widely used in England.

English textile manufacturers, rivals of the New Englanders both in world markets and in America, obtained their raw materials free of duty. There were good reasons for northeastern producers to believe that only the American system of imposts kept them from equaling the British in world trade. By the 1850's, many American mills had been in operation for three generations. They had experienced managers and weavers, cheap and abundant credit, modern machinery and production methods. In cotton cloth manufacturing, for which machinery could be used most extensively, New England labor was the most productive in the world. By 1860, the average number of looms per weaver was four in America, two in Great Britain. French and German manufacturers lagged even farther behind in methods an machinery.

In addition to high productivity which made their goods competitive in the world markets, and the need to import cheap raw materials, many New England manufacturers preferred low tariffs from a fear that high textile duties would foster the growth of new competitors at home. New producers might bring cutthroat competition and periodic chaos to the industry by their poor judgment of market conditions. A special committee of the Boston Board of Trade acknowledged in 1858 that New England textile manufacturers had potentially dangerous rivals, especially in Pennsylvania; but the committee concluded that the tariff reduction of 1857 removed any immediate threat. "Under the impulse of a high protective tariff they accomplished so little, that now, under a change of policy, there seems no present cause of alarm." When the higher Morrill duties came before the House in 1860, Representative Alexander H. Rice of Massachusetts, speaking for the manufacturers of his state, declared that "excessive protection" would stimulate "ruinous and irresponsible competition at home." In the Senate, textile manufacturer Henry Wilson proclaimed: "A high protective policy . . . is calculated to raise up rivals at home, and is more injurious to us than foreign competition."

After the war, fear of the growth of protected competition continued to influence New England tariff sentiment. Edward Atkinson, president of the Cotton Spinners of New England, and a director of the Boston Board of Trade, wrote to Henry Wilson in 1866: "The strongest men in the trade are more afraid of the unskillful competition built up at home by high duties than they are of foreign competition." Enoch R. Mudge, one of the most influential New England textile men, told the organizing meeting of the National Association of Cotton Manufacturers and Planters in 1868: "When we speak of protection, I think it should be given only at the point where the cotton manufacturer requires it." For well-established, efficient New England producers, of course, there were comparatively few points at which protection was necessary. They had seen evidence of the success of their low tariff theories in the few years the 1857 schedules were in force. "The operation of the tariff of 1857 has contributed largely to the prosperity of our woolen manufacturers," one of Boston's largest wool dealers reported in 1859. Exports of cotton cloth had risen steadily, from an average of $7,000,000 in the years 1851 through 1856, to almost $11,000,000 in 1860.

The government's need for revenue allowed protectionists an almost unchallenged ascendancy during the Civil War, but the battle between northeastern business groups over tariff schedules was resumed after Appomattox. For example, when a resolution for lower tariffs was placed before the National Board of Trade Convention in 1869, delegates from the Boston Board of Trade and Boston Corn Exchange voted 6 to 1 for the resolution; Philadelphia delegates voted 7 to 0 against it. The Boston Board of Trade also worked unsuccessfully to prevent abrogation of the reciprocity treaty with Canada; Philadelphia's Board joined western agricultural interests in demanding an end to reciprocity.

These divisions within the business community were likewise reflected in the congressional debates and voting on important tariff schedules. Cotton manufacturers resumed their prewar demands for lower schedules, even for cotton textiles. Senator William Sprague, whose sprawling Rhode Island mills were relatively inefficient, protested against the 25 per cent cut in cotton textile duties proposed in 1867. He was answered by Senator William P. Fessenden of Maine, sponsor of the measure: "I am informed

by the commissioner [Revenue Commissioner David A. Wells] that these duties were fixed at a rate perfectly satisfactory to those engaged in the manufacture of cottons, who appeared before him. . . . The cotton interest of this country has got so that it can stand of itself pretty much."

Schedules on coal similarly came under attack. As power looms replaced hand looms, and steam power replaced water power, New England manufacturers became increasingly interested in lower coal duties. Under reciprocity and the low tariff of 1857, imports of coal into Boston rose steadily from 88,531 tons in 1858, to 209,225 tons in 1865, most of this being cheap Nova Scotia fuel. Representative George S. Boutwell and Senator Charles Sumner of Massachusetts tried in vain to prevent higher coal schedules from being placed in the proposed tariffs of 1866 and 1867. Sumner acknowledged that there was a lot of coal in Pennsylvania, West Virginia, and the West. "But why," he asked, "should New England, which has a natural resource comparatively near at home, be compelled at a great sacrifice to drag her coal from these distant supplies?" Sumner's amendment was defeated 11 to 25, with eight New Englanders, both New Yorkers, and one senator from Oregon comprising those favoring lower duties on coal.

Many other schedules in the proposed bills of 1866 and 1867 were fought out by competing or conflicting business interests. Manufacturers, especially New Englanders, dependent upon cheap imported raw materials, were continually in opposition to the combined efforts of raw material producers and competing manufacturers closer to these native sources of supply. When Senator Benjamin F. Wade of Ohio moved to raise the duty on linseed, largely grown in the West, Fessenden of Maine accused him of asking the higher rate "for this simple, selfish reason: that the trade of crushing seed and manufacturing oil on the sea-coast may be utterly destroyed for the benefit of crushers of seed and the manufacturers of oil in the West."

Rolling mills, chiefly eastern, which controlled the American Iron and Steel Association, almost forced through an extremely low duty on scrap iron. Such a duty would allow the mills to import huge quantities of cheap European used rails, and to re-roll them in lieu of using domestic pig iron for new rails. Senator Zachariah Chandler, from the iron producing state of Michigan, demanded that the proposed duty on wrought scrap iron be quadrupled, and the duty on cast scrap be almost tripled. Lower schedules, he declared, would close the iron mines, put out every blast furnace, and mean "total ruin to the iron interests of the United States. . . . It is a bill gotten up to suit the railroad rolling-mills, and to sacrifice every other iron interest in the United States." The rolling mills won one Senate vote, but Chandler forced another, which was won by those sympathetic with the mine operators and pig iron producers. Almost all the western senators and both Pennsylvanians voted for higher duties on scrap metal. All but one senator from New England and New York voted for the low schedule.

The only tariff adjustment besides the wool and woolens bill to become law in the early postwar years was a measure passed in 1869, greatly increasing the duties on copper. Eastern smelters, who used a combination of eastern and cheap South American ores, were forced out of business by this bill, passed for the benefit of Lake Superior mine operators, whose domestic ores did not require smelting. The Lake Superior mine owners, some of whom were eastern financiers, were thus given a monopoly of the American market. They were thereby enabled to charge much higher than world prices at home and to dump their surplus abroad at much lower prices. Similar conflicts among business interests developed on tariff schedules for salt (used for scouring wool), zinc, lead, nickel, and building stones.

The wool and woolens bill of 1867, which considerably raised most schedules, has been cited as a prime example of the co-operation of business interests, because it was devised in a conference between a committee of wool growers and representatives of the National Association of Wool Manufacturers. What has generally been overlooked is the fact that the manufacturers' association, like the American Iron and Steel Association, was dominated by a well-organized segment of the industry, in this case by worsted and carpet manufacturers, whose interests conflicted with those of other important groups within the woolen industry.

Most influential of the men who negotiated the agreement for the manufacturers were Erastus B. Bigelow, president and founder of the Association, and America's leading carpet manufacturer; John L. Hayes, permanent secretary of the Association; and J. Wiley Edmonds, treasurer of the giant Pacific Mills, a leading worsted producer. Hayes reported to the membership that "for six months Mr. Bigelow gave himself unremittingly to the great work . . . [and to him they] must attribute the happy results of the conference." Before this "happy" conclusion, Hayes conceded, most woolen manufacturers "were becoming more and more disposed to look abroad for the chief supply of raw material . . . and were inclined to advocate the British policy of free trade in raw materials, including wool." Certainly the results of the conference were not so happy for manufacturers of woolen cloth, the largest item of domestic woolen output. These producers would be forced to pay much higher rates for imported raw wool than the worsted manufacturers with whom they competed. Carpet and blanket manufacturers would pay by far the lowest rates.

The largest manufacturer of wool cloth taking part in the negotiations with the growers was Edward Harris of the Harris Manufacturing Company, Woonsocket, Rhode Island. Harris later declared that he had no part in deciding the schedules, and that his name had been appended to the agreement without his knowledge or consent. Senator Henry Wilson of Massachusetts, a manufacturer of fine woolen cloth, told the Senate Finance Committee that if the new schedules were put into effect, he would have to close his factory. He subsequently declared in the Senate: "Some of the very ablest men in Massachusetts and in New England earnestly believe that this bill, so far as it concerns two thirds of the woolen manufacturers of the country, is not so good as the present tariff. [Only] the carpet manufacturers are abundantly satisfied." Wilson's statement was reinforced by other New England senators. William Sprague of Rhode Island, William P. Fessenden of Maine,

and Lot M. Morrill of Maine reported similar opinions of the wool and woolens bill among the cloth manufacturers in their constituencies. Nevertheless, there was no organized opposition in Washington to the energetic Hayes or to the large number of western congressmen who were anxious to honor an agreement which gave protection to wool growers. The wool and woolens bill passed easily despite adverse votes from men like Wilson, Sumner, and Sprague who had close associations with the New England woolen industry.

Northeastern opposition to the cloth schedules continued after the passage of the bill, and in the winter of 1869–1870, Edward Harris and forty-three other New England woolen manufacturers petitioned Congress to reduce the duties on wool for cloth as low as carpet wool duties, which were one-fifth as high. On reaching Washington with this petition, Harris was informed that the wool growers and John Hayes, who said he represented three hundred companies and individuals associated with the woolen industry, had first claim on congressmen's votes. In 1889, the woolen cloth manufacturers obtained 530 signatures from wool manufacturers and dealers asking for lower duties—and again failed. Finally, in 1909, the cloth manufacturers formed a separate organization to do permanent battle in Washington with the worsted and carpet interests.

For somewhat different reasons a low-tariff sentiment similar to that in New England was also strong in New York City, by far the largest importing and financial center in the country. New York merchants, shippers, and those who financed their activities opposed tariffs which might restrict imports, while the railroad financiers protested that under the proposed tariff of 1866 the Erie and the New York Central systems alone would have to pay out annually "about two million dollars by way of protection." The New York Chamber of Commerce had opposed the Morrill bill of 1861 as "a radical change in the tariff policy of the country," but had patriotically refrained from strenuous protests as tariff rates steadily rose during the war. In listing the organization's postwar objectives, however, Secretary John Austin Stevens declared: "The principles of free, unshackled trade, which it has ever upheld, must be reaffirmed." A few months after the war's end, the *Commercial and Financial Chronicle* observed: "Signs are not wanting that the subject of Free Trade will be made the text of the next political agitation in this country." The *Journal of Commerce* also began agitating for lower tariffs soon after the war; and the introduction of the first postwar tariff bill, providing for generally increased rates, naturally brought a strong protest from the New York Chamber of Commerce.

Clearly, then, New England cotton manufacturers and many wool and other manufacturers preferred and worked for lower tariff schedules—as did most of New York's financial and mercantile community. This fact was obvious to contemporary protectionists, especially the fervent Pennsylvanians. They recognized the role New Yorkers and New Englanders played in reducing many schedules, and in defeating, by obstructionist tactics, bills of which they disapproved. A delegate from Philadelphia's Board of Trade complained to the National Board of Trade in 1869 that New

England's industries had been built up behind tariff walls. "Now they are marked disciples of free trade. . . . They overlook the interests yet in their infancy. . . . Is this right? Is this just?" Henry C. Carey, leading spokesman for Pennsylvania iron, coal, and other protected interests, charged in 1867 that for twenty years, on tariff questions, "It has pleased the representatives of Massachusetts to array themselves on the side of cotton planters, slave owners, railroad monopolists."

Northeastern businessmen were thus far from united in support of high tariffs after the Civil War. Leading business interests of New England and New York believed that they lost more than they gained from high postwar tariffs. Had reconstruction politics allowed them a choice, it seems likely that these important groups would have preferred a return to the coalition which had produced the low tariff of 1857—a coalition which included the South. Certainly they would not have opposed the return of southern representatives in order to retain high imposts.

The business interests of the Northeast were divided into fiercely competing groups not only by the tariff issue, but by currency questions as well. . . .

From evidence such as this, the reconstruction program of the Radicals cannot be explained as an organized attempt by the business interests of the Northeast either to preserve and promote their own economic advantages or to obtain protection for economic exploitation of the South. Actually, northeastern businessmen had no unified economic program to promote. Important business groups within the region opposed each other on almost every significant economic question, and this lack of a common interest was likewise reflected in the economic views of Radical congressmen. Thaddeus Stevens, for example, dominant Radical leader in the House, was a fervent protectionist and a proponent of paper money inflation; Charles Sumner, Senate Radical leader, spoke and voted for lower tariff schedules and for resumption of specie payments. With both the businessmen and the legislators thus divided on economic issues, and with the New York merchants and financiers—who were in a position to gain most from economic exploitation of the South—definitely critical of the Radicals' program, it seems clear that factors other than the economic interests of the Northeast must be used to explain the motivation and aims of Radical Reconstruction.

1 This is the conclusion of the most recent survey of historians' attitudes toward Radical Reconstruction. T. Harry Williams, "An Analysis of Some Reconstruction Attitudes," *Journal of Southern History* (Baton Rouge), XII (November, 1946), 470. Williams calls this the "Beale thesis," because it has been most completely developed by Howard K. Beale in his

The Critical Year: A Study of Andrew Johnson and Reconstruction (New York, 1930), and his "On Rewriting Reconstruction History," *American Historical Review* (New York), XLV (July, 1940), 807–27.

2 William B. Hesseltine, "Economic Factors in the Abandonment of Reconstruction," *Mississippi Valley Historical Review* (Cedar Rapids), XXII (September, 1935), 191.

3 Helen J. and T. Harry Williams, "Wisconsin Republicans and Reconstruction, 1865–1870," *Wisconsin Magazine of History* (Madison), XXIII (September, 1939), 17–39.

4 For recent expressions of the "Beale thesis," see C. Vann Woodward, *Origins of the New South, 1877–1913* (Baton Rouge, 1951), 23–24; George R. Bentley, *A History of the Freedmen's Bureau* (Philadelphia, 1955), 34–36; William B. Hesseltine, *Confederate Leaders in the New South* (Baton Rouge, 1950), 136; Arthur S. Link, *American Epoch: A History of the United States since the 1890's* (New York, 1955), 4–5; George R. Woolfolk, *The Cotton Regency: The Northern Merchants and Reconstruction, 1865–1880* (New York, 1958).

Earlier statements of the thesis may be found in Charles A. and Mary R. Beard, *The Rise of American Civilization* (2 vols., New York, 1927), II, Chap. XX; Louis M. Hacker, *The Triumph of American Capitalism* (New York, 1940), Chap. 25; Richard N. Current, *Old Thad Stevens: A Story of Ambition* (Madison, 1942), Introduction, Chap. IV, and pp. 226, 249, 260; Matthew Josephson, *The Politicos, 1865–1896* (New York, 1938), Chap. I. James S. Allen, *Reconstruction: The Battle for Democracy, 1865–1867* (New York, 1937), is a Marxist version of the thesis.

Dissenting from the conclusions of Beale and Rhodes, LaWANDA (b. 1909) and JOHN H. (b. 1907) COX, professors of history at Hunter and City colleges respectively, maintain that the majority of Republicans supported the campaign to accord the freedmen equal legal rights. The Coxes were awarded the Dunning Prize in 1964 for *Politics, Principle, and Prejudice, 1865–1866*, and have written articles on the Freedmen's Bureau. In the following selection they explore the Negrophobia and partisan-political aims of Johnson and his followers. Like Rhodes, they are critical of the leadership exercised by President Johnson, but the reader will find a significant difference in their rationale.*

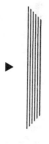

Civil Rights: The Issue of Reconstruction

No oratory of Charles Sumner, no lash of Thaddeus Stevens' tongue nor of his reputed political whip, could drive the Republican majority in Congress into sustained open warfare with the President. This accomplishment was Johnson's own. By refusing Presidential support to any program that would effectively secure equality before the law to the four million slaves whom the national government had made free, he fatally alienated the reasonable men who wished to act with him rather than against him. For some, the principle of equal status was decisive; for others, the prospect of repudiation by their Republican constituencies may have been sufficient reason. Johnson might have called for modified civil rights legislation or asked for a constitutional amendment to put beyond question the right of Congress to secure for the freedmen civil equality. He did neither.

By giving countenance to the Democratic claim that the Civil Rights Act was unconstitutional, Johnson helped to destroy any possibility that the civil rights issue, as Senator [Edwin D.] Morgan had hoped, would be removed from the political arena. When Congress

* Reprinted with permission of The Free Press from *Politics, Principle, and Prejudice, 1865–1866: Dilemma of Reconstruction America* by LaWanda and John H. Cox. Copyright © 1963 by The Free Press of Glencoe, a division of The Macmillan Company. Pp. 202–213, 231–232. Footnotes omitted.

subsequently formulated its own amendment, with the vital section one on citizenship and equal rights, Johnson might have accepted it in whole or in part, or he might have used it as a point of departure for compromise. Instead, the President made clear his disapproval of any constitutional amendment whatsoever before the South had been fully restored to a voice in national affairs. It was obvious at the time, as it is evident in retrospect, that no civil rights amendment could have received the requisite two-thirds vote of both Houses of Congress with the South fully represented. Neither in March of 1866, nor later, did Andrew Johnson give to the moderates of the party that had elected him any alternative with which they might spare the nation a dread conflict between Congress and the Chief Executive.

In declaring war upon the Radicals, Johnson chose to make as well an issue with moderate Republicans. His action on the Civil Rights Bill, like that on the Freedmen's Bureau Bill, cannot be explained on the sole basis of Radical provocation or constitutional principles. It must be viewed in the context of pressures from the Democracy, North and South, and of plans to precipitate a reorganization of national parties that would result in a new or transformed Union party under his personal leadership. Yet a new or transformed Union party would be only the Democracy in disguise unless it could command the support of moderate men in the Republican ranks. Whether Johnson wished the substance or only the appearance of a new amalgam, we cannot know. If the former, his unyielding attitude on the civil rights issue was a major blunder.

He may have been blinded by his own racial attitudes or by his victory in the battle over the Freedmen's Bureau Bill. Contemporary evidence, however, should have made unmistakably clear the near unanimity of Republican public opinion on behalf of some national guarantee of equal civil rights for the freedmen.

The advice of Henry Ward Beecher, of [Ohio] Governor [Jacob D.] Cox, of Thurlow Weed, and of Secretary Seward indicated the importance of the civil rights issue to continued support from rank-and-file Republicans. Even Senator [Edgar] Cowan in advising the second veto cautioned the President to "Be careful to put it distinctly as a question of *power*—not of policy—indeed it might be recommended to the States with propriety." It will be recalled that John Cochrane, who had labored so diligently to prepare the way for a Johnson party centered about the War Democrats, had sent similar advice. He had cautioned Johnson that in the approaching conflict with his "disguised enemies" it would be essential that the line of Presidential policy could not be interpreted as unfriendly to the Negro. "That concession to public opinion" would enable Johnson to carry the North. R. P. L. Baber, a diligent Johnson political lieutenant, wrote from Ohio both before and after the veto to Senator [James R.] Doolittle, Secretary Seward, and the President about the strategy needed for success in the approaching congressional elections. A central requisite was "Some effective and Constitutional law to enable the Freedmen to enforce in the Federal Courts, rights denied them in the State Courts, as to the protection of person and property." Russell Houston, an old personal friend who had acted as an intermediary between Johnson and the New York Democracy, wrote Johnson from Kentucky advising that the President's supporters in Congress take the lead in advocating a civil rights bill that would not be unconstitutional or inappropriate. "It is important to you and to the country, that when the issues now being made, shall go before the people, you should appear as you are and have been, the advocate, the friend and the promoter of the freedom of all the people of our Country whether of one race or another. . . . Under ordinary circumstances, I might say that no legislation on the subject was necessary, but under present circumstances, I think differently." A New Jersey representative wrote the President to explain that his vote on the Civil Rights Bill did not indicate any desire to desert the Administration. "Whilst a different course would not have sustained you practically it would have been a violation of my own sense of right, and in decided contravention of the will of our friends whose opinion I have ascertained by personal observation during my stay at Trenton last week. They strongly desire protection to the freedmen and fear the States would be slow to accord it."

Private letters to Secretary Seward and to Senator Morgan bear eloquent testimony to the importance of the civil rights issue. Seward's public defense of the Freedmen's Bureau veto evoked from an old friend and political supporter words of harsh but sorrowful repudiation. "Had any one predicted even a single year ago you would in so brief a period be found side by side with the Hoods, Vallandigham, Pearce, Buchanan, Voorhees, Brooks, Davis and

other aiders and abetters of the rebellion, I should have deemed him as a libeller. . . . [Your friends] have the painful mortification of seeing you co-operating with your life-long enemies and the enemies of Freedom, Justice, Humanity and the Union, to fasten upon the country a system of slavery ten times more odious and cruel than that which the Army of the Republic has destroyed." After the second veto, another former admirer wrote: "Your former friends are all deserting you. . . . Your reconstruction policy is believed by the people fatal to the true interests of liberty and the life of the Nation. Justice to the loyal whites of the South and the Freedmen is justice to the nation, so the people believe." The pastor of New York's Trinity Church wrote to commend Morgan for sustaining the Civil Rights Bill. "That Bill seemed to us to be the necessary Legislation to give vitality to the late Amendment to the Constitution of the United States and to make freedom a real thing to the emancipated. . . . It is high time to assert by Legislation, the Union and Nationality of this great Country, and to maintain the citizenship of every native born American." Another minister expressed satisfaction in the passage of the law for much the same reasons: "If our people are not to be protected by national law in the Civil Rights that are secured even in the empires of Europe, with what face can we stand up among the free nations of the world?" A New York banker succinctly stated the issue: "The Freedmen's Bureau Bill involved a question of expediency about which earnest Union men might differ—the Civil Rights Bill however stood upon a different basis. The people whose rights as

Citizens are sought to be protected by the Bill, were entitled to receive from the Government a law that would secure to them the practical enjoyment of those rights." A New York lawyer congratulated Morgan upon his vote: "I am not radical but I am confident you will never regret the aid you gave to common humanity in sustaining that bill."

The response of the press also indicated that Republican opinion was committed to some form of civil rights action. Republican papers were much more united in their support of Congress than had been the case after the first veto. [William Cullen] Bryant's *Evening Post*, which had supported the President earlier, now regretfully dissented. The moderate and conciliatory editor of the Springfield *Republican* reluctantly concluded that the Civil Rights Bill must be passed over the President's veto "or the hope of any special legislation for the protection of the freedmen must be abandoned." A few days later, at the very time when Senator Morgan was seeking compromise, [Samuel] Bowles wrote an extended analysis of the political situation. The President's purpose, according to the Springfield *Republican's* editor, had been to drive off from the Republican party a small faction of extreme radicals and consolidate the mass of Republicans with War Democrats of the North and loyalists of the South into a powerful party that would bring the Union "peace and prosperity" and "give him a triumphant re-election." Even after the February 22 speech, the President might have held half the Republicans, "led Congress to his plan of reconstruction," and gained a larger power with the country than he had ever before possessed. The veto of the Civil Rights Bill, however, "instead of driving off from him a small minority of the republican party, or even the half of it, drives off substantially the whole of it. There is but one voice among republicans on this point. . . . If Mr. Johnson is to stand by the doctrine of that document, he must inevitably part company with all the great body of his old supporters, and rely for his friends upon the northern democrats and the reconstructed rebels of the South. . . . For though they might give up everything else; waive universal suffrage, concede the admission of southern Congressmen, abolish the test oath, grant general amnesty, they cannot give up national protection to the weak and minority classes in the South." The *Democrat and Free Press* of Rockland, Maine, gave a similar warning. "Mr. Johnson is mistaken if he supposes that fanaticism is at the bottom of the movement to give the negroes the rights of free men. It is not fanaticism, but cool judgment; it is not sustained by the few, but by the great mass of those who fought down the rebellion." The Columbus, Ohio, *Journal* commented that by the veto, the President "had done more to strengthen the supporters of Congress and to determine the policy of the wavering, than months of argument."

Even the Republican papers that remained friendly in their attitude toward the President made clear their own support for some form of national guarantee of the freedmen's rights. A few reconciled their own attitude with that of the President by pointing to his concluding promise, the one Johnson had incorporated from Seward's draft, and insisting that the President was not opposed to Federal protection. Most of the Republican press, however, saw the veto as drawing a sharp line between the position of the President and that of their party.

What had been taking place in the Republican party since the close of the civil conflict was a gradual metamorphosis, similar to the one that had taken place during the war. The war years transformed the Republicans, a political amalgam originally united on the principle of opposition to the extension of slavery, into a party committed to the destruction of slavery. This objective had been formally embodied in the party platform of 1864. The platform, however, had not included a plank supporting equal legal status for the freed slaves, despite the fact that such a plank was offered and considered. By the winter of 1865, Republicans generally had expanded their repudiation of slavery into a condemnation of legal discriminations which by then seemed to them the last vestiges of slavery. Important elements within the party held that the freedmen's rights must include an equality of suffrage, but on this more advanced position, Republicans were not yet agreed. They had, however, come to identify Republicanism with a defense of basic civil rights for the freed slave. Sometimes this identification of Republicanism with the principle of equal status before the law was stated explicitly; sometimes it was expressed through generalizations that invoked liberty, freedom, or humanity. A characteristic argument, advanced by one Republican paper, was that if the position on equal civil rights embodied in Johnson's veto message were correct, then "all the principles of democracy and freedom upon which our creed of

Republicanism rests are false and we must recant them." When Republicans accused Johnson of treachery to the Republican party and Republican principles, or with greater forbearance simply asked that he give them some unmistakable evidence so that they might "continue to confide in him as a *Republican*," they were identifying their party with the principle of equality in legal status for all freedmen.

Thus what had once been an advanced, or "Radical," position within Republican ranks, by 1866 had become accepted and moderate. To most opponents of equal civil status, however, the principle still appeared "Radical." Herein lies one clue to the confusion in the use of the term "Radical" which plagues any serious student of the period. The term is inescapable; yet a man labeled a "Radical" by one set of contemporaries or historians is often found designated a "moderate" by another group of contemporaries or historians. All would agree that Charles Sumner, Thaddeus Stevens, and Wendell Phillips, extreme men though not of one mind, were the prototypes of Radicalism. The term *radical*, however, has often been used to identify, and castigate, all Republican opponents of Andrew Johnson. Many of these men were almost as critical of Sumner, Stevens, and Phillips as were their Conservative adversaries. Few followed Stevens in his demand for confiscation; most were ready to abandon or drastically compromise Sumner's aim of Negro suffrage. Though they wished to proceed with caution, there was no strong desire among them for an indefinite postponement of restoration by reducing the South to the status of "territories" or "conquered provinces."

In other words, many Radicals were moderate men. The Radical opponents of President Johnson were united in one demand—that of national protection for the freedmen. On other issues of Reconstruction they held widely divergent views.

It has sometimes been assumed that a common economic attitude united Radicals and marked them off from pro-Johnson men. This assumption is demonstrably false. Some were protariff men, some antitariff men; some advocated cheap money, some upheld a sound gold standard; some were spoilsmen, others were among the spoilsmen's bitterest critics. In 1865 and 1866 substantial members of the business community were as often found in the ranks of the President's supporters as in those of the opposition. John A. Dix, a key figure in the Johnson movement, was president of the Union Pacific. A twenty-thousand dollar reception and dinner at the famed Delmonico's, at the opening of Johnson's ill-fated Swing-around-the-Circle, was attended by many of the most powerful figures of New York business and finance. As late as September, 1866, the New York *Times*, in an editorial entitled "Business and Politics—the Conservatism of Commerce"—spoke of the "great unanimity of the commercial and business classes in supporting the conservative policy of the Administration, and in opposing with their might the schemes of the Radical Destructives."

Nor were the Radicals distinguishable from the general run of Union men, as is often claimed, by vindictiveness toward the South or clamor for the heads of "traitors." Indeed, New York's outstanding Radical leader, Horace Gree-

ley, was a leading figure in the movement for amnesty and forgiveness. Henry Wilson, Radical senator from Massachusetts, wrote to Johnson in support of a plea for the parole of Clement C. Clay of Alabama. Even Thaddeus Stevens offered his services in the defense both of Clay and of Jefferson Davis. The feeling against Southern leaders of the rebellion, which found expression both in a stubborn indignation at the prospect of their speedy return to the halls of Congress and in an emotional demand for Jefferson Davis' trial and conviction, cut across the division between pro-Johnson and anti-Johnson men. Thus in December, 1865, the House passed a resolution supporting the stringent Test Oath of July, 1862, as binding without exception upon all branches of government. Only one Republican registered opposition. A few days earlier, without a single dissenting voice, the House had declared treason a crime that should be punished; thirty-four Democrats joined the Republicans in voting "yea." In June, after the break with the President, a resolution calling for the trial of Jefferson Davis passed by a vote of 105 to 19, with no Republican voting against it. Six of the seven Conservatives who had broken with the majority of their party to support Johnson in the Civil Rights veto, registered their approval of this demand.

The only common denominator that united the Radicals of 1866, and the only characteristic they shared which could logically justify the term *radical*, was their determination that the rebel South should not be reinstated into the Union until there were adequate guarantees that the slaves liberated by the nation should enjoy the rights of free men. It is true that Johnson's opponents believed Congress should have some voice in Reconstruction and that they were profoundly disturbed by the prospect of a restored South, united with the Northern Democracy, immediately controlling the destinies of the nation. They were also extremely sensitive to any patronage moves that might seem to indicate Johnson's support of the Democracy or an intent to punish Republicans for failure to agree completely with the President's position. These attitudes, however, can hardly be termed radical; and they were not decisive factors with most of the men who broke with the President after the veto messages. Possibly, without the civil rights issue, one of these points of friction might have generated warfare and become the dividing line between Johnson's opponents and his supporters; but this is extremely doubtful. The testimony of such men as Samuel Bowles, Thurlow Weed, Jacob D. Cox, and John Cochrane must be given weight. They believed that the President could achieve his goal of speedy restoration and renewed fellowship between North and South if only he endorsed some effective national guarantee of the freedmen's civil rights as citizens. One of the most distinguished students of congressional Reconstruction, thoroughly sympathetic to Johnson, concluded that the moderate leadership in Congress desired just three conditions and would have settled for two: a guarantee of "the negroes' civil rights" and recognition of "the prerogative of Congress." Since executive action alone could not guarantee the South's permanent acquiescence in the freedmen's newly gained rights, such security could be had only by way of

the second condition, acceptance of some congressional action in the matter. In other words, the two conditions were inseparable; Johnson's consent to the first would have automatically fulfilled the second. Had Johnson come to terms with the moderates on the civil rights issue, the truly radical men of the party would have been clearly distinguishable from Republicans generally; and the true "Radical" would have faced the choice of compromise or defeat. Instead, except for a handful of Conservatives who totally accepted Johnson's leadership, "Republican" tended to become synonymous with "Radical."

The Democracy had a major responsibility for the blurring of distinction between the terms *Radical* and *Republican*. Even before the vetoes, they had tended to stigmatize the entire Republican leadership in Congress as "Radical"; after the vetoes, they delighted in maligning the Freedmen's Bureau Bill and the Civil Rights Act as parts of a sinister Radical design to defeat Johnson's plan for speedy restoration. This was good political strategy. Political expediency and propaganda, however, are not a complete explanation. In the eyes of Democrats, North and South, the claim of "equality," in any form, for the newly freed Negro was indeed radical, an outrageous postwar version of prewar Abolitionism. Both before and after the vetoes, one finds expressions in the Democratic press and in private letters of the period which indicate an unmistakable identification of "Radical" with "Abolitionist." Thus, a Tennessee judge, complaining about the interference of the military, started to write that this was "just what the abominable Abolitionis [*sic*]" desired, then crossed out "Abolitionis" and substituted the word "Radicals." It is true that Northern Democratic spokesmen and responsible Southerners at times urged upon the Southern states full equality in civil proceedings; but they did so because this appeared to them not only an inescapable concession to Republican opinion but a necessary condition for Presidential support as well. Moreover, so long as exclusive state authority were maintained, concessions made by state action before restoration could be undone by state action after restoration.

There is a certain validity in the Democratic equation that denied the historical differences between oldtime Abolitionists, postwar extremists, and those moderate Republicans of 1866 who upheld equal civil rights for the Negro. Between pro-Johnson Conservatives and anti-Johnson Radicals—whether the latter were moderate or extreme—the dividing line was marked by a distinction in race attitude. Wide differences existed on each side of the line, and there were those who took their places in each camp for reasons primarily of political expediency and advantage. Yet by 1866 all Radicals accepted, indeed most held as an article of faith, a nationally enforceable equality of civil status, even though their attitudes might differ in respect to equality of suffrage and equality of social status for the Negro. The position of Johnson supporters varied from extreme racism to an uncomfortable accommodation to the probability that legal discrimination and inequitable treatment for the freed slave would follow upon an unrestrained local autonomy in race relations. The anti-Johnson side attracted men with a deep sense of concern and responsibility for

the freed slave; the pro-Johnson ranks drew men who thought national responsibility had ended with the destruction of property rights in human beings. The latter preferred to base formal argument upon aversion to centralized government, a defense of states' rights, respect for the Constitution, and devotion to a reunited Union. But behind such arguments there most often lay some shade of that prejudice of race which still divides the nation.

The racist tendency among Northern Democrats hardly needs further demonstration. If evidence is desired, it can be found among the editorials with which the veto messages were greeted. Johnson does not believe, wrote one New England Democratic editor, "in compounding our race with niggers, gipsies and baboons, neither de we . . . [or] our whole Democratic people." A Washington paper editorialized:

The negro is to have full and perfect equality with the white man. He is to mix up with the white gentlemen and ladies all over the land . . . at all public meetings and public places he is to be your equal and your associate. . . . How long will it be if Congress can do all this before it will say the negro shall vote, sit in the jury box, and intermarry with your families? Such are the questions put by the President.

The *Ohio Statesman* declared it was no crime for the President to "esteem his race as superior to an inferior race. In this hour of severe trial, when the President is endeavoring so to administer the government that the white man shall not be subordinated to the negro race, will not the white man stand by him." The Radicals, commented a Pennsylvania paper with satisfaction, "now find that President Johnson regards this government as the White man's." . . .

In refusing to accept the equal rights provisions of the Civil Rights Act or of the Fourteenth Amendment, Johnson won lasting gratitude from white Southerners to whom the concept of equality between the races was anathema, and this despite the ordeal of military government and immediate universal Negro suffrage which they in all likelihood would have been spared had Johnson's course been different. But with this decision, the President lost the confidence and respect of moderate Republicans. Lyman Trumbull and John Sherman both felt a sense of betrayal in Johnson's veto of the Civil Rights Bill. "Besides," confided Sherman to his brother, "he [Johnson] is insincere; he has deceived and misled his best friends." The confidence in Johnson's assurances of justice for the freed people, which characterized Republican opinion, except that of extreme Radicals, in December, 1865, turned to distrust. No longer were misgivings directed toward Presidential policy alone; they came to embrace the President's intention and integrity, and corroded his public influence. "The truth is," Senator Fessenden wrote to Senator Morgan in mid-1867, "Mr. Johnson has continued to excite so much distrust that the public mind is easily played upon by those who are seeking only the accomplishment of their own purposes." By standing adamant against a federally enforceable pledge of minimum civil equality for the Negro as a prerequisite to restoration of the secession states, Johnson precipitated a great issue of moral principle central to the battle over Reconstruction; and he brought upon himself an unparalleled humiliation.

In the view of the early students of Reconstruction, Radical rule saddled the South with the most odious decade in its history. WILLIAM A. DUNNING (1857-1922), who taught at Columbia University and wrote numerous articles and monographs on Reconstruction, was one of the first historians to devote scholarly attention to Congressional Reconstruction. The following selection from his *Reconstruction, Political and Economic, 1865-1877* offers a classic statement of the "tragic era" thesis. Dunning describes a South subjected to the misdeeds of carpetbagger, scalawag, and Negro rule. For him, the period marked a low point in the history not only of the South but of the nation. While historians in the last few decades have disputed most of Dunning's conclusions, his position is important if for no other reason than because it is the interpretation still given in many textbooks used on all school levels.*

The Tragic Decade

The process of creating a new electorate and through it a new government in each of the ten states was carried on by the district commanders in close conformity with the radical spirit of the reconstruction acts. The registration of voters was so directed as to insure beyond all peradventure the fullest enrolment of the blacks and the completest exclusion of disfranchised whites. When the returns were all in it appeared that the negroes were in the majority in South Carolina, Alabama, Florida, Mississippi, and Louisiana, and the whites in Virginia, North Carolina, Arkansas, and Texas, while in Georgia the numbers were about equal. The first exercise by the newly enfranchised class of their high privilege was in the elections for the various constitutional conventions. In these elections, as in the registration, the military authorities assumed the duty of promoting in every way participation by the blacks, and of counteracting every influence tending to keep them from the polls. The result of the elections was a group of constituent assemblies whose unfitness for their task

* From William A. Dunning, *Reconstruction, Political and Economic, 1865-1877* (New York: Harper & Brothers, Publishers, 1907), pp. 111-112, 205-214. Footnotes omitted.

was pitiful. No one of them, indeed, lacked members of fair ability and creditable purpose; but the number of such members was small, and they were for the most part entirely out of touch with the intelligent and substantial classes of the population for whom they were framing a government. The chief part was taken in the conventions by northern men who had come South with the army or with the Freedmen's Bureau. Some few well-qualified native southerners also, of the Unionist element which had been the basis of the presidential restoration, assumed a prominent position in the deliberations; but the mass of the delegates consisted of whites and blacks whose ignorance and inexperience in respect to political methods were equalled only by the crudeness and distortion of their ideas as to political and social ends. . . .

The most conspicuous feature of maladministration was that of the finances. To the ambitious northern whites, inexperienced southern whites, and unintelligent blacks who controlled the first reconstructed governments, the grand end of their induction into power was to put their states promptly abreast of those which led in the prosperity and progress at the North. Things must be done, they believed, on a larger, freer, nobler scale than under the debased régime of slavery. Accordingly, both by the new constitutions and by legislation, the expenses of the governments were largely increased: offices were multiplied in all departments; salaries were made more worthy of the now regenerated and progressive commonwealths; costly enterprises were undertaken for the promotion of the general welfare, especially where that welfare was primarily connected with the uplifting of the freedmen. The result of all this was promptly seen in an expansion of state debts and an increase of taxation that to the property-owning class were appalling and ruinous. And the fact which was of the first importance in the situation was that this class, which paid the taxes, was sharply divided politically from that which levied them, and was by the whole radical theory of the reconstruction to be indefinitely excluded from a determining voice in the government.

Of the objects of outlay which contributed to swell the annual deficit of the state treasuries, many were, of course, unexceptionable from any point of view. The rebuilding of roads, bridges, and levees, the renovation of public offices and other property, the restoration of town improvements that had suffered by the devastation of the war—all these works absorbed large sums and were unopposed by the conservatives, save where extravagance and corruption were manifest or suspected. In respect to the blacks, the governments had now to assume many responsibilities which in slavery either pertained to the masters or had no existence. Thus the administration of criminal justice for the newly enfranchised citizens and the regulation of their family and property relations made an important increase of public expenditure inevitable. One of the largest items in the budgets of reconstruction was the schools. Free public education existed in only a rudimentary and sporadic form in the South before the war, but the new constitutions provided generally for complete systems on advanced northern models. The financial burden of these enterprises was very great, and the irritation thus caused was increased by the fact that the blacks were the chief beneficiaries of the new systems, while many of the white taxpayers considered the education of the negro, as carried on in the public schools, to be either useless or positively dangerous to society. . . .

In the maladministration that brought ruin to the finances, inefficiency and corruption played about equal parts. The responsible higher officials were in many cases entirely honest, though pathetically stupid, in their schemes to promote the interests of their respective states. But the governments numbered in their *personnel*, on the other hand, a host of officers to whom place was merely an opportunity for plunder. The progressive depletion of the public treasuries was accompanied by great private prosperity among radical politicians of high and low degree. First to profit by their opportunity were generally the northerners who led in radical politics; but the "scalawag" southerners and the negroes were quick to catch the idea. Bribery became the indispensable adjunct of legislation, and fraud a common feature in the execution of the laws. The form and manner of this corruption, which has given so unsavory a connotation to the name "reconstruction," were no different from those which have appeared in many another time and place in democratic government. At the very time, indeed, when the administrations of [Robert K.] Scott, in South Carolina, and [Henry C.] Warmoth, in Louisiana, were establishing the southern high-water mark of rascality in public finance, the Tweed ring in New York City was at the culmination of its closely parallel career. The really novel and peculiar element in the maladministration in the South was the social and race

issue which underlay it, and which came to the surface at once when any attempt at reform was instituted.

In most of the reconstructed states the very first term of the radical administration developed a schism in the party in power. In a general way the line of this cleavage was that dividing the southern white from the northern white element —the scalawag from the carpetbagger. Between these two elements there was a natural divergency of feeling and policy in respect to the blacks, who constituted the bulk of the party. As the negroes caught the spirit of politics and demanded more and more of the positions and essential power in their party, the southern whites could not bring themselves to the same amount of concession that the carpetbaggers made. The latter, therefore, became more and more decisively the controlling element of the party. Meanwhile the Democratic whites, constituting the main body of taxpayers, watched with deepest alarm the mounting debt and tax rate in every state. They were carrying most of the burden which radical extravagance and corruption were creating, and they had small chance of success in any election against the compact mass of negroes. They welcomed, therefore, the chance to profit by the radical schisms, and accordingly we find in most of the states, by 1872, a coalition of reforming Republicans and Democrats, under the name conservatives, in opposition to the dominant radicals. The net outcome of this movement was a sharpening of race lines in party division—a loss to the radicals of a considerable fraction of the initially small white element which they possessed. The tendency towards purely race parties was promoted also by the return to the North of many of the better class of carpetbaggers, discouraged with the failure of their projects for making an honest fortune.

. . . But the obstacles to a successful campaign against the radicals were appalling. Not only were the negroes impervious to arguments based on existing maladministration, but, where the whites were in the majority, the election laws of most of the states enabled the party in power to determine the result much at its will. In this matter the reconstructed constitutions and legislatures followed the example of the original acts of Congress, and conferred upon the governors much the same authority over the registration and elections as had been possessed by the district commanders during the military régime. Under cover of a purpose to insure protection to the negro voter, the control of the local electoral machinery was centralized at the state capitals, and extraordinary facilities for fraud were embodied in the laws regulating both the casting and the counting of the ballots. The capstone of the system was the "returning board," which in some of the states was so constituted and so endowed with power over the final canvass of the votes that the governor and his appointees could determine the result practically at their discretion, with but perfunctory reference to the earlier incidents of the election.

A final and terribly effective obstacle to political reformation by the conservatives was the power of the national administration. After the full committal of President Grant to the policy of the enforcement acts, the civil, judicial, and military service of the United States in the South became gradually a mere adjunct of the radical state governments. Energetically directed by the attorney-general at Washington, the district attorneys and marshals, and in some flagrant instances the district judges themselves, gave indispensable support to the radical cause. Indictments under the Ku-Klux act, never brought to trial, were used as a moderating influence on conservative enthusiasts in close districts; and it became a leading function of United States soldiers to counteract by their presence any tendency of negro interest in politics to wane. Thus the useful service of the national power in restraining the rash and violent elements of southern white society that were active in the later phases of the Ku-Klux movement was gradually transformed into the support of a social and political system in which all the forces that made for civilization were dominated by a mass of barbarous freedmen. . . .

The negro had no pride of race and no aspiration or ideals save to be like the whites. With civil rights and political power, not won, but almost forced upon him, he came gradually to understand and crave those more elusive privileges that constitute social equality. A more intimate association with the other race than that which business and politics involved was the end towards which the ambition of the blacks tended consciously or unconsciously to direct itself. The manifestations of this ambition were infinite in their diversity. It played a part in the demand for mixed schools, in the legislative prohibition of discrimination between the races in hotels and theatres, and even in the hideous crime against white womanhood which now assumed new meaning in the annals of outrage. But every form and suggestion of social equality was resented and resisted by the whites with the energy of despair. The dread of it justified in their eyes modes of lawlessness which were wholly subversive of civilization. Charles Sumner devoted the last years of his life to a determined effort to prohibit by Federal law any discrimination against the blacks in hotels, theatres, railways, steamboats, schools, churches, and cemeteries. His bill did not pass Congress till 1875, after his death, but his idea was taken up and enacted into law by most of the southern radical legislatures. The laws proved unenforceable and of small direct consequence, but the discussion of them furnished rich fuel to the flames of race animosity, and nerved many a hesitating white, as well as many an ambitious black, to violent deeds for the interest of his people.

The revisionists have brought into question the Dunning school's evaluation of the Negro voter and officeholder. A statement of this aspect of the revisionist position is given by JOHN HOPE FRANKLIN (b. 1915) of the University of Chicago. Franklin has written extensively on southern and Negro history. Among his works are *From Slavery to Freedom: A History of Negro Americans* (3d ed., 1967) and *The Militant South* (1956). A selection from one of his more recent works provides an interpretation in direct opposition to Dunning's. Franklin contends that the Dunning school has misrepresented the role of the Negro in Reconstruction. What weaknesses in Dunning's approach does Franklin exploit in reaching this conclusion?*

A Re-evaluation of Negro Participation

The entrance of Negroes into the political arena was the most revolutionary aspect of the reconstruction program. Out of a population of approximately four million, some 700,000 qualified as voters, but the most of them were without the qualifications to participate effectively in a democracy. In this they were not unlike the large number of Americans who were enfranchised during the age of Jackson or the large number of immigrants who were being voted in herds by political bosses in New York, Boston, and other American cities at this time. They were the first to admit their deficiencies. Beverly Nash, an unlettered former slave sitting in the South Carolina convention, expressed the views of many when he said: "I believe, my friends and fellow-citizens, we are not prepared for this suffrage. But we can learn. Give a man tools and let him commence to use them, and in time he will learn a trade. So it is with voting. We may not understand it at the start, but in time we shall learn to do our duty."

Like Nash most of the Negroes were illiterate. A slave existence could hardly be expected to prepare one for the responsibilities of citizenship, especially

* Reprinted from *Reconstruction After the Civil War* by John Hope Franklin, a volume in The Chicago History of American Civilization series, by permission of The University of Chicago Press. Copyright © 1961 by The University of Chicago. Pp. 86–92, 133–138.

when there were laws, as there were in all slave states, banning the teaching of slaves. Even if Negroes were free, as were more than 200,000 in the slave states before the war, laws forbade their being taught to read and write. Indeed, when they came out of slavery many Negroes did not know their own names; many did not even have family names. It goes without saying that a considerable number had not the vaguest notion of what registering and voting meant.

None of this is surprising. It had been only two years since emancipation from a system that for more than two centuries had denied slaves most rights as human beings. And it must be remembered that in these two years the former Confederates, in power all over the South, did nothing to promote the social and political education of the former slaves. What is surprising is that there were some—and no paltry number—who in 1867 were able to assume the responsibilities of citizens and leaders.

Among South Carolina's Negro leaders was state treasurer Francis L. Cardozo, educated at Glasgow and London, who had been a minister in New Haven and, after the war, was principal of a Negro school in Charleston. Robert B. Elliott, born in Massachusetts, trained at Eton College in England, and elected to Congress in 1870, was urbane and articulate. J. J. Wright, a state supreme court justice, had studied at the University of Pennsylvania and had been a respected member of the Pennsylvania bar before moving to South Carolina after the war. Congressman James Rapier's white father sent him to school in Canada, and when he returned to his native Alabama after the war he had not only an ample formal education but

a world of experience gained from travel and work in the North. Florida's secretary of state, Jonathan C. Gibbs, graduated from Dartmouth College and had been a Presbyterian minister for several years when reconstruction began. Among the Negro leaders of North Carolina James W. Hood, assistant superintendent of public instruction, and James H. Harris, an important figure in the 1868 constitutional convention, were educated, respectively, in Pennsylvania and Ohio. Many others, among them Henry M. Turner of the Georgia legislature, Hiram Revels, United States senator from Mississippi, and Richard H. Gleaves, member of Congress from South Carolina, had much more than the rudiments of a formal education when they entered upon their official duties.

Significant among Negro leaders were those who were almost wholly self-educated. Robert Smalls of South Carolina pursued his studies diligently until he had mastered the rudiments. Later he went to the United States House of Representatives. In Mississippi, John Roy Lynch regularly took time off from his duties in a photographer's studio to gaze across the alley into a white schoolroom, where he kept up with the class until he had mastered the courses taught there. When he became speaker of the Mississippi house and later a member of Congress, he relied on this earlier training. Before Jefferson Long went into Congress from Georgia, he had educated himself and had become a merchant tailor in Macon. There were numerous other self-educated Negro leaders, including John Carraway and Peyton Finley of Alabama, James O'Hara and A. H. Galloway of North Carolina, and James

W. Bland and Lewis Lindsay of Virginia. From this educated element came the articulate, responsible Negroes who contributed substantially to the writing of the new constitutions and the establishment of the new governments in the former slave states.

Most of the Negro leaders were ministers. A fair number taught school. Some were employees of the Freedmen's Bureau or another federal agency. Here and there one found a Negro who had been trained in the law. There were, of course, farmers; and there were some artisans engaged in a variety of occupations. The economic interests and aspirations of the Negro leaders varied widely. It would be wrong to assume that they had no economic interests or that they had no views regarding the economic future of the South.

One of the really remarkable features of the Negro leadership was the small amount of vindictiveness in their words and their actions. There was no bully, no swagger, as they took their places in the state and federal governments traditionally occupied by the white planters of the South. The spirit of conciliation pervaded most of the public utterances the Negroes made. In his first speech in the South Carolina convention Beverly Nash asserted that the Southern white man was the "true friend of the black man." Pointing to the banner containing the words "United we stand, divided we fall," Nash said, "If you could see the scroll of the society that banner represents, you would see the white man and the black man standing with their arms locked together, as the type of friendship and union which we desire."

Negroes generally wished to see political disabilities removed from the whites.

In South Carolina several Negroes presented a resolution asking Congress to remove all such disabilities, and it was passed. In Louisiana the Negroes requested that former Confederates be permitted to vote but, for the time being, not to hold office. In Alabama James T. Rapier, a Negro delegate to the constitutional convention, successfully sponsored a resolution asking Congress to remove the political disabilities of those who might aid in reconstruction. In Mississippi a Democratic paper, the Jackson *Clarion*, admitted that in their general conduct Negroes "have shown consideration for the feelings of the whites. . . . In other words, the colored people had manifested no disposition to rule or dominate the whites, and the only Color Line which had existed, grew out of the unwise policy which had previously been pursued by the Democratic Party in its efforts to prevent the enjoyment by the newly-emancipated race of the rights and privileges to which they were entitled, under the Constitution and laws of the country." In South Carolina Beverly Nash declared that in public affairs "we must unite with our white fellow-citizens. They tell us that they have been disfranchised, yet we tell the North that we shall never let the halls of Congress be silent until we remove that disability."

Negroes attempted no revolution in the social relations of the races in the South. Francis B. Simkins in his "New Viewpoints of Southern Reconstruction" has accurately observed that "the defiance of the traditional caste division occasionally expressed in an official reception or in an act of the legislature was not reflected generally in common social relations." Negroes, as a rule, conceded to the insistence of whites that they were a race apart; and they made little or no attempt to invade social privacies. They did not even attempt to destroy white supremacy except where such supremacy rejected Negroes altogether as human beings, and there was almost nowhere any serious consideration given to providing legal approbation of interracial marriages. While Negroes sought equality as human beings, they manifested no desire to involve themselves in the purely social relations of whites as individuals or as groups. "It is false, it is a wholesale falsehood to say that we wish to force ourselves upon white people," declared the near-white P. B. S. Pinchback of Louisiana.

Nor did any considerable number of Negroes seek to effect an economic revolution in the South. Henry McNeal Turner, the fearless Negro leader who was almost universally disliked by white Georgians, did what he could to assist the whites in recovering their economic strength. In the Georgia convention he secured the passage of two resolutions that indicated a remarkable willingness to stabilize the economic life of the white community. One sought to prevent the sale of property whose owners were unable to pay their taxes; the other provided for the relief of banks. In South Carolina Negro leaders such as Robert DeLarge and Francis Cardozo supported relief measures with the full knowledge that whites would benefit as much as Negroes. . . .

No group has attracted more attention or has had its role more misrepresented by contemporaries and by posterity than Southern Negroes during Radical Reconstruction. The period has been described as one of Negro rule, as one of

gross perfidy with the Negro as the central figure, since the reins of misgovernment were supposedly held by black militiamen. Negroes were not in control of the state governments at any time anywhere in the South. They held public office and, at times, played important parts in the public life of their respective states. But it would be stretching a point to say that their roles were dominant, and it would be hopelessly distorting the picture to suggest that they ruled the South. It was in South Carolina that they had the greatest numerical strength. In the first legislature there were eighty-seven Negroes and forty whites. From the outset, however, whites controlled the state senate and in 1874 the lower house as well. At all times the governor was white. There were two Negro lieutenant governors, Alonzo J. Ransier in 1870 and Richard H. Gleaves in 1872. There were other Negro leaders. Samuel J. Lee was speaker of the House in 1872 and Robert B. Elliot in 1874. From 1868 to 1872 Francis L. Cardozo was secretary of state, and from 1872 to 1876 he was state treasurer. Jonathan J. Wright, a member of the Pennsylvania bar before coming to South Carolina, sat on the state supreme court for seven years, but he was the only Negro to achieve a judicial position of that level in any state.

Despite their large numbers, 437,400 compared to 353,800 whites in 1860, Negroes in Mississippi did not approximate a numerical domination of the state government. In the first reconstruction legislature there were 40 Negro members out of a total of 115. According to John R. Lynch, Negro speaker of the house in 1872, "Of seven state officers, only one, that of Secretary of State, was filled by a colored man, until 1873 when colored men were elected to three of the seven offices." They were A. K. Davis, lieutenant governor, James Hill, secretary of state, and Thomas W. Cardozo, superintendent of education. Of the situation in 1873 Lynch declared, "Out of seventy-two counties in the State . . . electing on an average twenty-eight officers to a county, it is safe to assert that not five out of one hundred of such officers were colored men." Vernon Wharton, after a careful study of the problem, concludes that "although Negroes formed a majority of the population in thirty counties in Mississippi, they almost never took advantage of their opportunity to place any large number of their race in local offices."

Several Louisiana Negroes were prominent and influential, but they never approached a dominant position in public affairs. The forty-two Negroes in the first legislature were in the minority, as were the Negroes in succeeding legislatures. Three Negroes served as lieutenant governor: Oscar J. Dunn, 1868–1871; P. B. S. Pinchback, 1871–1872, who acted as governor for forty-three days in 1872 when Governor Warmoth was ousted; and C. C. Antoine, 1872–1876. Other Negroes held important offices, including P. G. Deslonde, secretary of state, 1872–1876; Antoine Dubuclet, state treasurer, 1868–1869; and W. G. Brown, superintendent of public education, 1872–1876. Most of the Louisiana Negro leaders had been free before the war and had enjoyed some educational opportunities. Of the seven Negroes in the state senate in 1868 only one, Oscar J. Dunn, had been a slave; and before the war he had purchased his own freedom. Pinchback, a

well-to-do former captain in the Union army, had been educated in Cincinnati. He had the physical appearance of a white man but his white skin gave him little advantage in the hurly-burly of reconstruction politics in Louisiana.

In the other state governments the roles of Negroes were even less significant. In the North Carolina legislature they constituted barely one-seventh of the membership, and the only Negro official of any consequence was James Walker Hood, who served as assistant superintendent of public instruction for several years. The first Alabama legislature saw only twenty-six Negroes out of a total membership of eighty-four, and there were no important state offices in the hands of Negroes. The "horrors of Negro domination" from which Alabamans prayed deliverance simply did not exist. James T. Rapier is the only Negro who was at all prominent; after serving as assessor of internal revenue in Alabama he went on to Congress. What influence Negroes might have had in Georgia was nullified by their expulsion from the legislature. By the time they returned, Radical Reconstruction had been so effectively undermined that there was little chance for Negroes to exert any considerable influence.

Florida had only nineteen Negroes in its first legislature, which contained seventy-six members. Their influence was extremely limited. The only high-ranking Negro in the state government was Jonathan C. Gibbs, who was secretary of state from 1868 to 1872 and superintendent of public instruction from 1872 to 1874. Very few Negroes held other than minor offices in the new government in Virginia. Twenty-seven sat in the first legislature, and there were none among the policy-makers in the executive branch of the government. The influence of Negroes in Arkansas was meager. At the beginning of the period none held any important offices. In 1871 W. H. Grey was appointed commissioner of immigration, a position he held until 1873. J. C. Corbin, a graduate of Oberlin College, served as superintendent of education from January, 1873, to October, 1874. There were no important Negro officeholders in Texas, but G. T. Ruby of Galveston wielded considerable political influence, while Norris Wright Cuney, also of Galveston, held several offices, including membership on the county school board and state inspector of customs.

In a different but highly significant category were the sixteen Negroes who served in Congress between 1869 and 1880. Two of them, Hiram R. Revels and Blanche K. Bruce, represented Mississippi in the Senate. Revels was a North Carolina free Negro who had lived in several Northern states and had studied at Knox College in Illinois. By the time of the Civil War he had become an ordained minister in the African Methodist Episcopal Church and had taught school in several places. During the war he recruited Negroes for the Union army, founded a school for freedmen in St. Louis, and joined the army as chaplain of a Negro regiment in Mississippi. At the war's end he settled in Natchez, entered politics, and in 1870–1871 filled the Senate seat previously held by Jefferson Davis. Bruce had been born a slave in Virginia. When war came he escaped to Missouri and soon was teaching Negroes in Hannibal. After the war he studied in the North for several years and went to Mississippi

in 1869. Soon he got into politics and worked up from tax collector to sheriff to county superintendent of schools. In 1875 he went to the United States Senate, where he served a full term. His wide range of interests as a lawmaker is seen in his introduction of bills on the Geneva award for the Alabama claims, aid to education, railroad construction, and the reimbursement of depositors in the Freedmen's Savings Bank.

South Carolina sent six Negroes to the House of Representatives, the largest number from a single state. But they were not all in the House at one time. Alabama was second with three. Georgia, Florida, Mississippi, North Carolina, and Louisiana sent one each. Most of these men had some experience in public service before going to Congress. Alonzo Ransier of South Carolina had been a member of the constitutional convention, auditor of Charleston County, and lieutenant governor. John R. Lynch of Mississippi and James T. Rapier of Alabama had served their states in similar fashion. Some were war heroes, like Robert Smalls of South Carolina who had seized the Confederate ship "Planter" in 1862 and delivered it to Union authorities. In addition to representing their constituents in the usual ways, Negro members of Congress showed considerable interest in a wide range of national questions. Joseph Rainey of South Carolina and Josiah T. Walls of Florida were strong advocates of federal aid to education. John A. Hyman of North Carolina championed relief for the Cherokee Indians, while all were outspoken in their vigorous support of civil rights legislation. Their responsible conduct moved James G. Blaine, their contemporary, to observe,

"The colored men who took their seats in both Senate and House did not appear ignorant or helpless. They were as a rule studious, earnest, ambitious men, whose public conduct . . . would be honorable to any race."

Where Dunning sees only the retrogressive side of Congressional Reconstruction, JACK B. SCROGGS (b. 1919) finds that the Radicals made many valuable changes in southern law. Professor of history at North Texas State University and author of a number of articles on Radical Reconstruction, Scroggs analyzes the constitutional changes adopted by the carpetbagger conventions in the South Atlantic states. He introduces into the debate an interpretation that points up progressive and democratic aspects of the period. Particular attention should be given to this selection, because it provides a definite dissent from the conclusions of the Dunning school.*

Carpetbagger Constitutional Reform in the South Atlantic States

The reconstruction period brought to the south fundamental changes in state politics and in political theory, climaxing a strong ante bellum movement in this direction. Among the many changes produced by the social-political revolution of the postwar era were lasting constitutional reforms of a progressive and democratic nature. Not least responsible for this development were the newly arrived Northerners—the carpetbaggers, who, along with the Southern scalawags, have long borne the major blame for all Reconstruction ills in the South. Accused by contemporaries of every conceivable crime, both political and civil, the term *carpetbagger* even among recent writers has carried with it the taint of ineptness, fraud, and corruption. This has tended to obscure the basic contributions made by the Northern immigrants who engaged in politics and to distort the role of the new Republican organizations in the South.

Only of local importance during the early stages of Reconstruction, these Northern "adventurers" achieved a commanding position in state politics with the advent of Radical control of the Reconstruction program early in 1867.

* Jack B. Scroggs, "Carpetbagger Constitutional Reform in the South Atlantic States, 1867–1868," *Journal of Southern History*, XXVII (November, 1961), 475–493. Copyright © 1961 by the Southern Historical Association. Reprinted by permission of the Managing Editor. Footnotes omitted.

The triumph of the Radicals in Congress brought about in the South a corresponding emergence of state Radicals, both white and Negro, and the Republican party developed as a formidable force in the new Southern political orientation. The strength of these new political organizations was clearly demonstrated in the results of the constitutional convention elections of 1867 in the five South Atlantic states—Virginia, North Carolina, South Carolina, Georgia, and Florida. The delegates to these conventions were largely representatives of the Negroes and lower class whites, who, as it happens, composed the two segments of society most eager to secure constitutional reform. Although the carpetbaggers were never in a majority in these delegations, their influence on Southern politics reached its high point in the framing of the new constitutions.

The degree of carpetbagger leadership and influence in the constitutional conventions varied from state to state. In Virginia, North Carolina, and South Carolina, convention debates and proceedings were dominated by recently arrived Northerners. The same was true of the Florida convention, but internal party schism brought ultimate defeat to the Radical Republican element there. Georgia alone of the South Atlantic states was relatively free from carpetbagger influence in the formation of her new constitution.

An appraisal of the motives of the carpetbagger leaders in the state conventions is difficult except in terms of the final products of their deliberations. Political and economic self-interest doubtless dictated the moves of many of the key Republican leaders, but in the drafting of new constitutions instances of attempts to limit the political freedom of any segment of the population were rare. Indeed, the primary aim of the carpetbagger group was the extension of political democracy, the assumption being that with complete political equality for all men Republican principles would prevail and the Southern Republican party would capture and retain control of the state governments. Demonstrating a lack of understanding of Southern society and politics, a great many of these leaders were struggling to impose constitutional changes on a reluctant South simply because they considered the changes long overdue.

With control of three of the South Atlantic state conventions firmly lodged in the carpetbagger element, it was evident that fundamental changes would appear in the new constitutions of these states. Even in Florida and Georgia, where a certain amount of co-operation with native white Conservatives tended to alleviate the revolutionary nature of constitutional innovations, it was clear that a return to the *status quo ante bellum* would not suffice. Unlike the conventions of 1865 which had primarily aimed at making only required amendments to old constitutions, the conventions of 1867–1868 were to embark on a program of basic constitutional reform.

Liberal constitutional provisions embodying the ideal of democratic equalitarianism which had developed during the past half century formed the framework of the new instruments of government. Many of these provisions were copied from constitutions of Northern states, and the carpetbaggers, as one would expect, were generally foremost in their advocacy. The states with the most able carpetbagger leadership emerged with the most democratic and progressive constitutions, and, as able Northern leadership decreased, the liberality of the documents tended to decrease proportionally. The Southern Republicans of course understood that democratizing of government would serve to strengthen the voting elements upon which they depended while at the same time weakening the former Democratic leaders who, standing to gain nothing from constitutional change, were on record as favoring no further change, and were declaring the whole process of Reconstruction an unconstitutional abridgement of the South's rights.

When the constitutional conventions met in late 1867 and early 1868, they initially faced problems outside the realm of pure constitution-drafting. While the standing committees were preparing their reports, the convention sessions were taken up with the pressing matter of the people's destitute condition. The results of their deliberations were the passage of ordinances of relief, or stay laws, measures which the Radicals had freely promised in their campaign for control of the conventions. These ordinances intended to alleviate financial suffering were to remain in force only until adequate provisions could be inserted in the new constitutions.

The debate over a relief ordinance in the South Carolina convention disclosed a division in carpetbagger ranks in that state. Carpetbaggers William J. Whipper and Niles G. Parker were the principal supporters of a temporary relief measure, basing their argument on the assumption that the legislation they favored would not only protect debtors but also those laborers who were dependent upon property owners for wages. In opposition, Negro carpetbaggers Richard H. Cain and Francis L. Cardozo maintained that by refraining from passing a relief act the convention would force the large plantation owners to sell their holdings and thereby permit the poor people of the state to purchase small farms. Whipper's answer to this was that "it would be perfect folly to entertain the opinion that in the present miserable destitution of the South the poor people will become the owners of the vast tracts of land if thrown into the market." He alleged that another consideration prompted the opponents of the ordinance when he joined native Negro R. C. De Large in asserting that a great part of the opposition was initiated by Northern and local investors who would be able to buy up the estates and become "large land monopolists." The dispute was resolved when General E. R. S. Canby issued a general relief order for the Carolinas, but the South Carolina convention carried relief further by declaring all contracts and liabilities for the purchase of slaves null and void.

In North Carolina the question of relief initiated a vigorous debate over the constitutional status of the state itself, with the carpetbagger leaders displaying a considerable divergence of opinion. Albion W. Tourgée maintained the "old North Carolina was dead and buried in the tomb of the Confederacy." From a territorial status she must be brought back to statehood with adequate homestead provisions to protect the mass of people. Tourgée's constitutional position led naturally to his support of repudiation of the old state debt, but the convention refused to back him in this.

In all of the South Atlantic states

the conventions incorporated into the new constitutions permanent relief measures under the provisions protecting homesteads, which had the advantage of avoiding the odium attached to the term "stay laws." These liberal homestead provisions assured the citizen of retaining in his possession a minimum amount of property by exempting it from attachment for debts. Although an innovation in these states, homestead provisions provoked little opposition from any quarter, the only controversy developing over the amount of the exemption. The Radicals wished to make the exemption large enough to protect the small owners but not so large as to give protection to owners of large landholdings. North Carolina and South Carolina, following the leadership of the carpetbaggers, limited their homestead exemption to a moderate $1,500, while Florida provided for the exemption of $1,000 in personal property and one hundred and sixty acres in land, or one acre within the limits of an incorporated town. Virginia gave a larger exemption, real and personal property to the value of $2,000; and the Georgia convention under the sway of conservative business men and planters led by Joseph E. Brown and Rufus Bullock, gave the largest exemption, real and personal property to the value of $3,000. Other relief provisions were put into the new constitutions. In Georgia, for instance, a sweeping relief ordinance was included in the constitution over the protests of the Democrats who questioned its constitutionality and charged that the forces of Brown and Bullock designed it as a snare to catch the ignorant debtor.

In view of subsequent developments, of particular interest is the movement which developed in the conventions for specific provisions for the payment of the state debts and for limitation of state aid to companies and corporations. All of the conventions acknowledged responsibility for the old state debts, excepting war debts. Tourgée, the Ohio carpetbagger in North Carolina, opposed the payment of the state debt, arguing that since the war had left North Carolina in a territorial status, the old state debt had already ceased to exist, despite the demand of Northern speculators that it be paid. For his stand in favor of repudiation Tourgée was vigorously attacked by fellow Northerners in the convention, as well as by the Conservative press. With the entire carpetbagger element opposing him Tourgée lost his fight on the repudiation issue. He subsequently led in the movement for prompt payment of the state debt, and the convention passed an ordinance which provided for the payment of the interest due on state bonds and for the funding of the debt in new six per cent state bonds.

All five conventions set limitations upon the use of public credit. In South Carolina carpetbagger Niles G. Parker, chairman of the finance committee, presented a report which called for limiting the state debt to $500,000 and for prohibiting the legislature from extending the state credit to the aid of any private company. The North Carolina convention forbade the legislature to contract new debts except to supply a casual deficit or to suppress invasion or insurrection, unless the same bill included a tax to cover the deficit. Virginia went further in declaring the credit of the state would not "be granted to, or in aid of, any person, association, or corporation."

Both the Georgia and Florida conventions provided that the state credit could be used in support only of internal improvements and in no other cases.

The debates on the bills of rights in the conventions disclosed the determination of the carpetbaggers to incorporate in the new constitutions basic principles of equalitarianism despite the bitter opposition which greeted their attempts to eradicate the legal distinctions between the races. Only after a vicious parliamentary struggle did the carpetbaggers of North Carolina, in league with the Negro members, secure the adoption of a provision in the bill of rights stating that "all men are created equal." The South Carolina convention accepted an amendment offered by Negro carpetbagger B. F. Randolph which specifically forbade any distinction on account of race or color and provided that all citizens "enjoy all common, public, legal, and political privileges." The Florida and Georgia constitutions contained no specific guarantee of equal civil and political rights.

All of the bills of rights reaffirmed the right to *habeas corpus* and provided that henceforth no one was to be imprisoned for debt except in cases of fraud; and in North Carolina Tourgée secured the adoption of a section stating that no man would be "compelled to pay costs or jail fees, or necessary witness fees of the defense, unless found guilty." The bills of rights in the Virginia, North Carolina, and South Carolina constitutions had sections designed to prevent in the future the imposition of property qualifications for voting or for holding office, and carpetbagger S. S. Ashley secured the adoption of a section guaranteeing all people in North Caro-

lina the right to a public education. Finally, the bill of rights adopted in each of the state conventions except in Georgia declared that all rights not delegated by the constitutions were reserved to the people.

An important progressive measure sponsored by each convention was the establishment of a state controlled system of public education. It was generally conceded that improvements in public education were needed, but carpetbagger leaders were particularly active in fostering plans for raising the educational level of the South. Although there was no serious opposition in Virginia to a public school system, a bitter controversy developed over segregation of whites and blacks in a dual system. Extremists on both sides were silenced when the convention accepted a compromise offered by C. H. Porter from New York which evaded the issue by making no specific reference to either mixed or separate schools. In North Carolina liberal provisions for public education were sponsored by Ashley, chairman of the committee on education. Tourgée gave him valuable aid, at one time unsuccessfully trying to amend the finance section so as to allocate to educational purposes all funds received from the poll tax. In North Carolina, as in Virginia, Conservatives attempted to insert provisions for the establishment of separate schools for the two races, but no stipulation was made in the section on segregation as adopted. South Carolina carried the principle of equality even further by declaring that all public schools, colleges, and universities of the state would be open to all children and youth "without regard to race or color." Disagreement in South

Carolina came over the issue of compulsory attendance in the public schools, with C. P. Leslie opposing the greater part of the carpetbagger leadership in their promotion of compulsory education. Leslie took the occasion to deliver a denunciation of the Massachusetts members of the convention, but his fulminations failed to prevent the passage of the section requiring all children from six to sixteen to attend school for at least twenty-four months. Georgia and Florida followed the trend and adopted provisions calling for the establishment of a system of public schools and with no specific statement as to segregation of the races.

The conventions achieved other significant reforms. There was a general revision of the state penal systems with a lowering of the number of crimes punishable by death. Tourgée expressed the attitude of the Northern immigrants on penal reform when he said,

Not only is punishment to satisfy justice but to reform the offender. That . . . is the key-note of civilization. Now as we are laying slavery and all its concomitants . . . a higher and nobler penal system should be devised.

North Carolina, South Carolina, and Florida also made specific provisions for state penitentiaries. The constitutions of Virginia, North Carolina, and South Carolina included elaborate sections outlining the form of a new county-township government, and in all of the South Atlantic states except Florida provisions were made for the popular election of county officers. Local control of civil affairs was avowedly designed to stimulate the interest of the masses of people in government. Tax reforms provided for

by the new constitutions tended to shift the burden of taxation from individuals to the owners of property, and made taxes uniform throughout each state. Property rights of women were extended by providing that property in the possession of a woman at the time of marriage or acquired by her thereafter was not liable in payment of the debts of her husband.

In all five states, the new constitutions altered to a greater or lesser degree the structure of the three traditional branches of state government. The executive branch underwent drastic changes in two of the states, while the remaining three states retained vestiges of ante bellum centralization. In North Carolina the convention eliminated the old Executive Council, heretofore elected by the General Assembly, and over the protests of the Conservatives created four new elective positions: lieutenant governor, superintendent of public works, auditor, and superintendent of public instruction. The election of these officials, along with that of the secretary of state and attorney general, was placed in the hands of the voters. The tendency to make the officers of the executive department directly responsible to the people was evident in the constitution of South Carolina, but Georgia and Florida, under more Conservative influence, made all executive officers except the governor, and in the case of Florida, the lieutenant governor, either appointive by the governor or elective by the General Assembly. Virginia also reserved to the General Assembly the right to elect all executive officers except the governor and lieutenant governor. The period of required residence for election to the governorship was generally made low in order to assure the eligibility of the Northern newcomers, and each state abolished property requirements of candidates for the governorship. North Carolina Conservatives made determined efforts to retain a section requiring a freehold to qualify for governor, but in vain. The Conservative press was loud in its condemnation of the changes in the executive branch:

The whole tenor of the report . . . [the Raleigh *Sentinel* declared], smacks of Yankee manipulations, and ignores the safe and staid temper of the Old North State, which has always eschewed inducements to experiment, at the sacrifice of her conservatism and well-earned integrity.

The judicial branch of the new state governments reflected the extent of the tide of democratic thought. In North Carolina Tourgée, unable to persuade the judiciary committee to approve his proposals to have the people elect the judges and to abolish the distinction between suits at law and suits in equity, carried his fight to the convention floor and secured the adoption of both proposals. The North Carolina convention appointed Tourgée, Victor C. Barringer, and W. B. Rodman as commissioners to prepare rules of judicial procedure and to codify the laws under the changes adopted by the convention. The *Sentinel* branded the popular election of judges as "the most dangerous stride towards mobocracy yet made by the destructives"; and North Carolina was, in fact, the only state in the South Atlantic area to take so democratic a stand. South Carolina provided that the General Assembly elect judges; and, although definite terms of office were fixed for each of the court judges, the carpetbagger leaders were not completely satisfied. D. H.

Chamberlain declared that the "doctrine that the people are not to be trusted with the selection of those who are to administer justice to them, I believe to be wholly unfounded." Division among the carpetbagger leaders in South Carolina, however, prevented approval of popular election of judges even though one of their strongest leaders insisted in this connection that "the whole program of the age is in favor of removing power from the hands of the few, and bestowing it on the many." Virginia, like South Carolina, provided that the General Assembly elect her judges, but both Georgia and Florida eliminated any vestiges of local control of the judiciary by permitting the governor, with the consent of the senate, to appoint them. In fact the Georgia constitution, insofar as the judiciary was concerned, was less democratic than the constitution of 1865, which had provided for the election of supreme court judges by the General Assembly and lesser judicial officials by the voters. Carpetbagger A. L. Harris recognizing this retrogression protested against the enormous appointive power being concentrated in the chief executive. North and South Carolina abolished county and district courts, and all five states fixed the tenure of office for judges at a specific number of years.

There were far-reaching reforms incorporated in the provisions of the new constitutions dealing with the legislative branches and with the suffrage. After replacing North Carolina's ancient title of House of Commons with the more common House of Representatives, the North Carolina convention abolished property qualifications for membership in either house. The other four South Atlantic states continued to require no property qualifications for membership in either house. Virginia Radicals, however, inserted a section imposing the same disabilities for office-holding as were imposed by the Fourteenth Amendment, and the native whites in the Georgia convention, when considering a section of the report of the committee on franchise providing that "all qualified electors" should be eligible to hold office, persuaded the Negroes that they were eligible for office without this clause, and that its inclusion would only serve to make it more difficult to secure ratification of the constitution. The political trick worked; by a vote of 126 to 12 the section was dropped, and the only specific guarantee of the right of the Negro to hold office in Georgia was lost.

The liberalization of the qualifications for membership in the various general assemblies was effected with little difficulty, but on the long-standing question of the basis of apportionment the Conservatives waged a bitter battle. In North Carolina Conservative John W. Graham contended that unless the amount of taxes paid by a district were to be used in apportioning seats in the upper house in the time-honored manner, property would be left defenseless before the weight of sheer numbers. Carpetbagger John R. French gave voice to the more democratic view:

Our fathers wrought according to the light of their day, and have entered upon the reward of their honest toil. Another future opens before us. Not property, not a few families, however old, or however respectable, are to rule the North-Carolina of the hereafter—but the free and mighty people . . . these are to be her voters and her legislators.

The old rivalry between the Charleston area and the upcountry of South Carolina was revived in that state convention with the upcountry delegates expressing fear of continued low-country domination. In the three upper South Atlantic states the demands of the western areas were met by specific constitutional provisions of future apportionment of senators and representatives on the basis of population. Florida limited the number of representatives to four from any one county, and Georgia devised a complex system by which the state was divided into districts of three counties each for the purpose of electing senators; and in the apportionment of representatives the six largest counties were allowed three each, the thirty-one next largest, two each, and the remaining ninety-five, one each.

In the case of Florida the initial apportionment, and the limitation of representation from any one county to a maximum of four, meant that control would be assured for the whites, inasmuch as the Negroes were concentrated in the few populous counties. The Radicals tried to persuade Congress to disallow the second Florida constitution on the grounds that its legislature was unrepresentative, but their efforts were in vain. Similarly, the Georgia constitution achieved white control of the legislature by its system of geographic apportionment. Thus, the issue of representation was not entirely a continuation of the old struggle between democrats and aristocrats; Negro suffrage brought a new facet to the problem. As was true in Georgia and Florida, apportionment of seats in the legislature could be used as a means of maintaining white political supremacy.

The question of suffrage caused great apprehension among the Conservatives, and one reactionary organ predicted

that once the Republicans decreed suffrage to be an "inherent right" there
would remain "no security for the rights
of property, and every man will hold
whatever property he does hold at the
mercy of the rabble." But there was
never any real doubt in any of the states
about the inevitability of Negro voting,
and Negro suffrage was generally accepted by Conservatives in all of the
states except North Carolina as a necessity forced upon the states by an overbearing conqueror. In the Old North
State young Plato Durham and William
A. Graham resolutely opposed the universal manhood suffrage movement. Durham went so far as to press the issue by
early presenting resolutions which
stated that any attempt to abolish or
abridge the natural distinction between
the white and black race would be a
crime against civilization and God. The
resolutions were immediately tabled, but
the able young Confederate veterans,
who continued to harass the exponents
of universal manhood suffrage for the
remainder of the session, were able to
define the position of the Conservatives
in a minority report of the committee on
suffrage. "We do not regard the right to
vote as natural or inherent, but constitutional merely—to be regulated in such
way as will best promote the welfare of
the whole community." Durham and
Graham condemned the whole scheme
of universal manhood suffrage

as intended to advance party purposes, in
the expectation that the States of the South
being Africanized and Radicalized may
more than counterbalance the loss of
electoral votes . . . in other sections of the
Union.

Attempts to limit Negro suffrage in
this manner proved futile, and the sections of the new constitutions dealing
with the franchise all embodied the principle of universal manhood suffrage.
Radicals in the Virginia, North Carolina, and Georgia conventions sought to
restrict the franchise of former rebels,
but only Virginia placed restrictions on
former Southern leaders, and this was
done over the bitter opposition of some
of the leading carpetbaggers and against
the advice of General John M. Schofield.
Several of the South Carolina carpetbaggers favored the imposition of a poll
tax as a requirement for voting in order
to "instill into the minds and hearts of
the people the sacredness of the ballot-
box," and one South Carolina report on
suffrage would have required after 1875
an ability to read and write as a requirement for voting.[7] But the ideal of universal manhood suffrage exercised too great
a hold on the minds of the delegates to
allow any limitation on the right to
vote. With the exception of Virginia, all
of the South Atlantic states extended the
ballot to all males over twenty-one, born
or naturalized in the United States, who
had resided in their state for one year
(six months in the case of Georgia); and
all the constitutions except those of
Georgia and Florida guaranteed qualified electors the right to hold a state
office.

Conservative delegates in the three
conventions securely under carpetbagger
domination were powerless to stop the
changes instituted by the Northern "adventurers," but they persisted in offering
amendments supporting the "white
supremacy" position and used the debates on the convention floors to appeal
to native whites and arouse their fear of
Negro supremacy. William A. Graham,
for instance, attempted to secure passage
of an amendment to the section on

militia providing that no white North Carolinian would have to serve with a Negro or ever obey an order from a Negro. Young Plato Durham was more extreme in his demands that no Negro or anyone with Negro blood ever be eligible for the office of governor, lieutenant governor, or any other executive office, and that intermarriage between the "Caucasian and African races" be prohibited.

As has been seen, in the two states of Georgia and Florida where carpetbagger influence proved less effective and native white Conservatives or groups cooperating with them controlled the conventions, the resulting constitutions were relatively conservative. The apportionment of seats in the legislature assured continued white domination of the General Assembly, and the broad appointive power of the governor and legislature in each state, even on the local level, made for centralization of power. As long as the whites held the office of governor, they could effectively deprive the Negroes of any real share in state government. The constitutions of Georgia and Florida attest to the considerable confidence of the Conservatives in their ability to carry the forthcoming elections inasmuch as the technique could work in reverse if the Radicals captured control of the executive. The Florida constitution, even more clearly than that of Georgia, bears the stamp of Conservative influence. Some liberal constitutional reform was desired by Conservatives or Democrats in both states, but the Negro issue brought about a coalition of Conservative Republicans and former Democrats and Whigs dedicated to the maintenance of white supremacy at all costs.

Even so, constitutional changes adopted by the Reconstruction conventions of 1867–1868 made a sweeping extension of political democracy in the South Atlantic states. Except for the changed status of the Negro, the innovations represented reforms long sought and so designed to capture the support of a large number of Southern whites as well as the large new bloc of Negro voters. During the course of the ante bellum period the poorer classes of Southern whites had successfully fought for an extension of the franchise to all white adult males and, with less success, for equal opportunities of officeholding. The imposition of Congressional Reconstruction extended the sphere of democracy still further by according the franchise, and generally the right to hold office, to all adult men, including the Negro, and by retaining and enlarging the principles of earlier bills of rights. The constitutional conventions of Virginia, North and South Carolina based apportionment of representation upon population for the first time, extended popular control of local government, and made most offices, both state and local, elective rather than appointive.

The carpetbagger who successfully championed political democracy revealed no such enthusiasm for extending economic democracy. The Northern settlers in the South, whose respect for property rights precluded an extensive program of debt repudiation or property confiscation, seemed to have been convinced that the same industry and commerce which had transformed the North would revolutionize the South. One carpetbagger expressed his confidence that "the plaster of profit laid upon the sores of war would work a miraculous cure." Whenever Negro spokesmen did display a desire for radical economic measures, property-conscious Northerners and Southerners combined to block them.

The success of the Republicans in the South depended upon the adoption of major political changes, for without guarantees of continued political democracy the basis of Radical strength would be undermined; and Northern immigrants, the carpetbaggers, took the lead in providing for the South a democratic political structure. But time demonstrated that democratic institutions, too, were capable of manipulation.

KENNETH M. STAMPP (b. 1912) takes exception to Dunning's view of the carpetbaggers and scalawags. Professor of history at the University of California, Berkeley, and author of *The Peculiar Institution* (1956) and *And the War Came: The North and the Secession Crisis, 1860–1861* (1950), Stampp provides a synthesis of revisionist scholarship in *The Era of Reconstruction, 1865–1877* (1965). In a passage from that work, he argues that Radical rule must be examined not only within the broad framework of ante- and post-bellum southern history but in reference to national events. How does this approach lead Stampp to advance conclusions on carpetbagger-scalawag motives and actions at variance with those of Dunning?*

Radical Rule: The Tragic Decade Thesis Disputed

[T]he customary charges against the new southern leadership are extremely severe and need to be weighed carefully. It is essential, therefore, to examine in some detail each of the three elements in the radical coalition—the carpetbaggers, scalawags, and Negroes—to test the validity of the generalizations conservatives used to characterize them. The term "carpetbagger" was applied to recent northern settlers in the South who actively supported the radical Republicans. Since the term has an invidious connotation, it is used here only for lack of another that is equally familiar but morally neutral. The so-called carpetbaggers were not all poor men who carried their meager possessions with them in carpetbags; they were not all ignorant; they were not all corrupt. Rather, they were a heterogeneous lot who moved to the South for a variety of reasons.

Among the carpetbaggers were some who fitted the stereotype: disreputable opportunists and corruptionists who went south in search of political plunder or public office. Because these carpetbaggers were so conspicuous and gained such notoriety, conservative southern Democrats succeeded in portraying them

---

* From *The Era of Reconstruction* by Kenneth M. Stampp. © Copyright 1965 by Kenneth M. Stampp. Reprinted by permission of Alfred A. Knopf, Inc. Pp. 158–165, 173–185. Some footnotes omitted.

as typical, though actually they constituted a small minority.

Few of the carpetbaggers came to the South originally for the purpose of entering politics; many of them arrived before 1867 when political careers were not even open to them. They migrated to the South in the same manner and for the same reasons that other Americans migrated to the West. They hoped to buy cotton lands or to enter legitimate business enterprises: to develop natural resources, build factories, promote railroads, represent insurance companies, or engage in trade. A large proportion of the carpetbaggers were veterans of the Union Army who were pleased with the southern climate and believed that they had discovered a land of opportunity. Others came as teachers, clergymen, officers of the Freedmen's Bureau, or agents of the various northern benevolent societies organized to give aid to the Negroes. These people went south to set up schools for Negroes and poor whites, to establish churches, and to distribute clothing and medical supplies. They were of all types—some well trained for their jobs, others not. Seldom, however, can they be dismissed as meddlesome fools, or can the genuineness of their humanitarian impulses be doubted. But whether honest or dishonest, northern settlers who became active in radical politics incurred the wrath of most white southern conservatives. For their supreme offense was not corruption but attempting to organize the Negroes for political action.

A scalawag is by definition a scamp, and white Southerners who collaborated with the radicals were thus stigmatized by the pejorative term that identified them. In southern society, according to

one critic, scalawags constituted the "tory and deserter element, with a few from the obstructionists of the war time and malcontents of the present who wanted office."[1] But here, as in the case of the carpetbaggers, the facts were more complex than this. All scalawags were not degraded poor whites, depraved corruptionists, or cynical opportunists who betrayed the South for the spoils of office.

The cases of three distinguished scalawags will illustrate the inadequacy of any simple generalization about the character or origin of this class of radicals. The first is that of Lieutenant General James A. Longstreet of the Confederate Army, a graduate of West Point and one of Lee's ablest corps commanders. After the war Longstreet moved to New Orleans and became a partner in a cotton factorage business and head of an insurance firm. In 1867, arguing that the vanquished must accept the terms of the victors, he joined the Republican party and endorsed radical reconstruction. In 1868 he supported Grant for President, and in subsequent years Republican administrations gave him a variety of offices in the federal civil service. The second case is that of James L. Orr of South Carolina, a secessionist who had sat in the Confederate Senate. After serving as the Johnsonian governor of his state, Orr switched to the radicals and in 1868 was rewarded with a circuit judgeship. In a private letter he explained why he now supported the Republicans: It is "important for our prominent men to identify themselves with the radicals for the purpose of controlling their action and prevent-

[1] Walter L. Fleming: *Civil War and Reconstruction in Alabama* (New York, 1905), p. 402.

ing mischief to the state." The third case is that of R. W. Flournoy, a large slaveholder in ante-bellum Mississippi. Flournoy joined the radicals not for personal gain but because of a humanitarian interest in the welfare of the freedmen. In a letter to Stevens he once explained that he supported the Republicans as the party to whom the Negro "can alone look . . . for protection." Flournoy's support of racial equality made him one of the most hated scalawags in the state. None of these men fitted the scalawag stereotype.

Others unfortunately did. Among those who gave the scalawags their reputation for corruption was Franklin J. Moses, Jr., of South Carolina. The son of a distinguished father, Moses entered politics before the war and was known as an ardent secessionist. In 1867, after a brief period as a Johnsonian, he joined the radicals. Both as a legislator and, from 1872 to 1874, as governor he looted the public treasury and repeatedly accepted bribes for using his influence to secure the passage of legislation. Other scalawags appeared to be pure opportunists who simply joined the winning side. Joseph E. Brown, Georgia's Civil War governor, provides a classic example. After the war, claiming that he had sense enough to know when he was defeated, Brown quit the Democrats and urged Southerners to accept the radicals' terms. During the years of reconstruction, in addition to his political activities, he found the time (and the opportunity) to become a wealthy capitalist: president of a railroad, a steamship company, a coal company, and an iron company. When the radicals were overthrown in Georgia, Brown, as always, landed on his feet and returned

to the Democratic party. Now he helped to organize a powerful Democratic machine that dominated the state for many years and eventually sent him to the United States Senate.

Always a minority of the southern white population, more numerous in some states than in others, the scalawags usually belonged to one or more of four distinct groups. The first and largest of these groups was the Unionists. Having been exposed to severe persecution from their Confederate neighbors during the war, southern Unionists were often the most vindictive of the radicals; they were quite willing to support those who would now retaliate against the secessionists, and they hoped that congressional reconstruction would give them political control in their states. Early in 1866 a North Carolinian wrote Stevens that Union men were disillusioned with Johnson but still hoped "that traitors will be punished for the treatment that union men received at their hands."

However, a very large proportion of this Unionist-scalawag element had little enthusiasm for one aspect of the radical program: the granting of equal civil and political rights to the Negroes. They favored the disenfranchisement of the Confederates to enable them to dominate the new state governments, but they were reluctant to accept Negro suffrage. "There is some small amount of squirming about the privileges extended to the recent slaves," a Virginia Unionist informed Stevens, "but time will overcome all this as there is no union man who does not infinitely more fear and dread the domination of the recent Rebels than that of the recent slaves." In 1866, General Clinton B. Fisk, an officer of the Freedmen's Bureau, told the congressional Committee on Reconstruction that in Tennessee "among the bitterest opponents of the negro . . . are the intensely radical loyalists of the [eastern] mountain districts. . . . The great opposition to the measure in the Tennessee legislature, giving the negro the right to testify and an equality before the law, has come from that section, chiefly. In Middle Tennessee and in West Tennessee the largest and the wealthiest planters . . . have more cordially cooperated with me in my duties than the people of East Tennessee." The planters believed that they could control the Negro vote, and the scalawags feared that they would.

Insofar as there was any relationship between scalawags and the class structure of the South, it resulted from the fact that a minority of the poor whites and yeoman farmers were attracted to the radical cause. There had always been . . . an undercurrent of tension between them and the planter class, and some of them deserted President Johnson when it appeared that his program would return the planters to power. Lower-class whites who joined the radicals sometimes hoped for a seizure of the planters' lands. In South Carolina, according to a Union officer, the idea of confiscation "was received with more favor by this caste than by the Negroes." He recalled numerous occasions when "dirty, ragged, stupid creatures slyly inquired of me, 'When is our folks a-gwine to git the lan'?'" But it was never easy for the yeomen or poor whites to become scalawags, for support of the radicals meant collaboration with Negroes, or at least acquiescence in Negro suffrage. As a result, this class of scalawags was most numerous in areas with a small Negro population. Elsewhere a few lower-class

whites managed to submerge their race prejudice, but the great majority preferred the old conservative leadership to a party that seemed to preach equality of the races.

A third source of scalawag strength came from Southerners engaged in business enterprise and from those living in regions, such as East Tennessee, western Virginia and North Carolina, and northern Alabama, which were rich in natural resources and had an industrial potential. Among such men there was considerable support for the economic policies of the Republican party—for the national banking system, the protective tariff, and federal appropriations for internal improvements. In general, the radical governments invited northern capitalists to invest in the South, granted loans or subsidies to the railroads, and gave charters and franchises to new corporations. Some of the scalawags were thus identified with the concept of a New South whose economy would be more diversified than that of the Old.

Finally, the radicals drew a little of their scalawag support and some of their leaders from upper-class Southerners who had been affiliated with the Whig party before the Civil War. The Whig party had been particularly attractive to the more affluent and socially secure members of southern society, and after the war many Whigs were reluctant to join their old foes, the Democrats. A few of them now looked upon the Republican party as the heir to the Whig tradition and wondered whether it might be possible not only to join but also to control its organization in the South. Upper-class Whig scalawags found it relatively easy to accept equal civil and political rights for Negroes, first, because among them race hatred was less often the prime motivating force of political action and, second, because they were optimistic about their chances of controlling the Negro vote. In Mississippi, for example, James L. Alcorn, elected governor on the Republican ticket in 1869, had been a prominent Whig planter before the war, as had been numerous other leading scalawags. Thus it would appear that the scalawags were in part an absurd coalition of class-conscious poor whites and yeoman farmers who hated the planters, and class-conscious Whig planters and businessmen who disliked the egalitarian Democrats. But politics has a logic of its own, and the history of American political parties is full of contradictions such as this. . . .

At the time that the new constitutions were ratified, elections were held for state officers and legislators. After the elections, when Congress approved of the constitutions, political power was transferred from the military to the new civil governments. Thus began the era of radical government in the South—an era which, according to tradition, produced some of the worst state administrations in American history. Some of the southern radical regimes earned their evil reputations, others did not; but viewed collectively, there was much in the record they made to justify severe criticism. To say that they were not always models of efficiency and integrity would be something of an understatement. "The great impediment of the Republican party in this state," wrote a Tennessee radical, "is the incompetence of its leaders. . . . After the war the loyal people in many counties had no competent men to be judges, lawyers or political leaders." Indeed, all of the radical governments suffered more or less from the incompetence of some, the dishonesty of a few, and above all the inexperience of most of the officeholders. Unquestionably the poorest records were made in South Carolina during the administrations of the carpetbagger Robert K. Scott and the scalawag Franklin J. Moses, Jr., and in Louisiana during the administrations of the carpetbaggers Henry C. Warmoth and William P. Kellogg.

The sins of various radical governments included fraudulent bond issues; graft in land sales or purchases and in the letting of contracts for public works; and waste and extravagance in the use of state funds. Governor Warmoth was reputed to have pocketed $100,000 during his first year in office, though his salary was $8,000; another governor was accused of stealing and selling the supplies of the Freedmen's Bureau. A scalawag governor admitted taking bribes of more than $40,000; another fraudulently endorsed state bonds over to a group of railroad promoters. In Louisiana under both Warmoth and Kellogg there was corruption in the granting of charters and franchises, in the negotiation of construction contracts, in the use of school funds, in the collection of state taxes, and in the awarding of printing contracts. Some of the radical legislators, especially in South Carolina, apparently made bribery an integral part of the process of transacting legislative business. One South Carolina legislature issued bonds valued at $1,590,000 to redeem bank notes valued at $500,000; it voted a bonus of $1,000 to the speaker when he lost that amount in a bet on a horse race. For a time the legislators of this state enjoyed the services of a free restaurant and bar established for their private use; they billed the state for such "legislative supplies" as hams, ladies' bonnets, perfumes, champagne, and (for one unfortunate member) a coffin. The cost of state printing in South Carolina between 1868 and 1876 was greater than the cost had been from 1789 to 1868. On one occasion, as the legislature was about to adjourn, a Democratic newspaper in Charleston wrote the following epitaph: "In life it has been unlovely, and in death it has not belied its record. As it lived, it has died—an uncouth, malformed and abortive monstrosity, its birth a blunder, its life a crime, and its death a blessing."

Meanwhile, the credit of some of the southern states was impaired as public debts mounted. In Florida the state debt increased from $524,000 in 1868 to $5,621,000 in 1874. In South Carolina a legislative committee reported that between 1868 and 1871 the state debt had increased from $5,403,000 to $15,768,000, but another committee insisted that it had increased to $29,159,000. By 1872 the debts of the eleven states of the former Confederacy had increased by approximately $132,000,000. The burden on taxpayers grew apace. Between 1860 and 1870 South Carolina's tax rate more than doubled, while property values declined by more than fifty per cent. In Tennessee a radical reported that during the first three years after the war taxes had increased sevenfold, though property had declined in value by one third. Throughout the South the tax burden was four times as great in 1870 as it had been in 1860. Such rates, complained many southern landholders, were confiscatory; and, indeed, taxes and other adversities of the postwar years

forced some of them to sell all or part of their lands. Sympathy for South Carolina's planter aristocracy caused a northern conservative to ask: "When before did mankind behold the spectacle of a rich, high-spirited, cultivated, self-governed people suddenly cast down, bereft of their possessions, and put under the feet of the slaves they had held in bondage for centuries?"

High taxes, mounting debts, corruption, extravagance, and waste, however, do not constitute the complete record of the radical regimes. Moreover, to stop with a mere description of their misdeeds would be to leave all the crucial questions unanswered—to distort the picture and to view it without perspective. For example, if some of these governments contained an uncommonly large number of inexperienced or incompetent officeholders, if much of their support came from an untutored electorate, there was an obvious reason for this. Howard K. Beale, in a critique of various reconstruction legends, observed that the political rulers of the antebellum South "had fastened ignorance or inexperience on millions of whites as well as Negroes and that it was this ignorance and inexperience that caused trouble when Radicals were in power. . . . Wealthy Southerners . . . seldom recognized the need for general education of even the *white* masses."[2] Even in 1865 the men who won control of the Johnson governments showed little disposition to adopt the needed reforms. In South Carolina the Johnsonians did almost nothing to establish a system of public education. and at the time that the radicals came to power only one

[2] Howard K. Beale: "On Rewriting Reconstruction History," *American Historical Review*, XLV (1940), pp. 807–27.

eighth of the white children of school age were attending school. The Negroes, of course, had been ignored entirely. It was probably no coincidence that the radicals made their poorest record in South Carolina, the state which had done the least for education and whose prewar government had been the least democratic.

As for the corruption of the radical governments, this phenomenon can be understood only when it is related to the times and to conditions throughout the country. One must remember that the administrations of President Grant set the moral tone for American government at all levels, national, state, and local. The best-remembered episodes of the Grant era are its numerous scandals —the Crédit Mobilier and the Whiskey Ring being the most spectacular of them —involving members of Congress as well as men in high administration circles. There were, moreover, singularly corrupt Republican machines in control of various northern states, including Massachusetts, New York, and Pennsylvania. But corruption was not a phenomenon peculiar to Republicans of the Gilded Age, as the incredible operations of the so-called Tweed Ring in New York City will testify. Indeed, the thefts of public funds by this organization of white Tammany Democrats surpassed the total thefts in all the southern states combined.

Clearly the presence of carpetbaggers, scalawags, and Negroes in the radical governments was not in itself a sufficient explanation for the appearance of corruption. The South was being affected by the same forces that were affecting the rest of the country. No doubt the most important of these forces were, first, the social disorganization that accom-panied the Civil War and hit the defeated and demoralized South with particular severity; and, second, the frantic economic expansion of the postwar period, when the American economy was dominated by a group of extraordinarily talented but irresponsible and undisciplined business leaders. These entrepreneurs' rather flexible standards of public morality provided an unfortunate model for the politicians.

Whether southern Democrats would have been able to resist the corrupting forces of the postwar decade had they remained in power is by no means certain. Perhaps the old ruling class would have been somewhat less vulnerable to the temptations of the Gilded Age, but the record of the Johnson governments was spotty at best. In Louisiana the conservative government created by Lincoln and Johnson wasted a great deal of public money. In Mississippi the state treasurer of the Johnson government embezzled $62,000. (This, by the way, far surpassed the record of the only thief in the radical government, who embezzled $7,000.) E. Merton Coulter discovered that during the era of reconstruction some Democratic officeholders "partook of the same financial characteristics as Radicals" and "took advantage of openings" when they found them. He quotes a Georgia editor who claimed that the extravagance and corruption "benefitted about as many Democrats as Republicans"; and he notes that a Democratic administration in Alabama "in lack of honesty differed little from the administrations of the Radicals between whom it was sandwiched."[3]

In the 1870's, when the South's so-

[3] [E. Merton] Coulter, *The South during Reconstruction*, [1865–1877 (Baton Rouge, 1947)] pp. 152–153.

called "natural leaders" returned to power, that troubled section did not always find itself governed by politicians distinguished for their selfless devotion to public service. In Mississippi the treasurer of the Democratic regime that overthrew the radicals in 1875 immediately embezzled $316,000, which broke all previous records! Elsewhere in the next decade eight other state treasurers were guilty of defalcations or embezzlements, including one in Louisiana who defrauded the state of more than a million dollars. Georgia was now ruled by a Democratic machine that was both ruthless and corrupt, a machine whose record was so offensive that by the end of the 1880's the white masses—some even willing to accept Negro support—rose in political rebellion against it. Reports about the Mississippi Democratic regime of the late nineteenth century are particularly colorful. One white editor charged that an "infamous ring" of "corrupt office-seekers . . . [had] debauched the ballot boxes . . . incurred useless and extravagant expenditures, raised the taxes, [and] plunged the State into debt." At the Mississippi constitutional convention of 1890, a white Democratic delegate gave the following description of politics in his state during the previous fifteen years: "Sir, it is no secret that there has not been a full vote and a fair count in Mississippi since 1875. . . . In other words we have been stuffing ballot boxes, committing perjury, and here and there in the state carrying the elections by fraud and violence. . . . No man can be in favor of perpetuating the election methods which have prevailed in Mississippi since 1875 who is not a moral idiot." Twelve years later an editor claimed that it would tax "the range and

scope of the most fertile and versatile imagination to picture a condition of greater political rottenness" than existed in Mississippi at that time.

In the final analysis the crucial question about the extravagance and peculations of the radical governments is who the chief beneficiaries were. Only a few of the Negro and white radical leaders profited personally. The funds they stole, the money that prodigal legislators used for their own benefit, accounted for only a small fraction of the increased debts of the southern states. Nor did the total sums involved in bribery rise to a very impressive figure. And why was the tar brush applied exclusively to those who accepted the bribes and not to those who offered them? Under these circumstances is it really more blessed to give than to receive? For when the bribe-givers are identified we have located those who profited most from radical misdeeds. These men were the construction contractors, business speculators, and railroad promoters, or their agents, who hoped to persuade legislators to give them contracts, franchises, charters, subsidies, financial grants, or guarantees. They were the men who were also corrupting Congressmen and northern legislatures.

In Virginia much of the history of reconstruction concerns the rivalry of the Baltimore and Ohio Railroad and the Southside line for control of the Virginia and Tennessee Railroad. Both lines fought to control elections and legislators and backed whichever party promised to serve them, until, in 1870, the legislature ended the dispute by approving the consolidation plans of the Southside. Louisiana's reconstruction politics was enlivened by the attempt of a railroad and steamship corporation, headed by Charles Morgan of New York, to prevent the state from subsidizing a rival line between New Orleans and Houston, until Morgan forced the new line to take him in. In Alabama the North and South Railroad and the Alabama and Chattanooga Railroad battled for access to the ore deposits around Birmingham. In the process the competing groups corrupted both Johnson and radical legislatures, and in the latter both Republicans and Democrats.

Most of the debt increases in the southern states resulted not from the thefts and extravagance of radical legislators but from the grants and guarantees they gave to railroad promoters, among whom were always some native white Democrats. In Florida more than sixty per cent of the debt incurred by the radical regime was in the form of railroad guarantee bonds. In North Carolina the radical government, prodded by the carpetbagger Milton S. Littlefield, a skilled lobbyist, issued millions of dollars of railroad bonds. Among those who benefited were many of the state's "best citizens," including George W. Swepson, a local business promoter and Democrat. Most of Alabama's reconstruction debt —$18,000,000 out of $20,500,000—was in the form of state bonds issued to subsidize railroad construction, for which the state obtained liens upon railroad property. When one measure for state aid was before the Alabama legislature, many Democrats were among the lobbyists working for its passage. Yet, complained a radical, the Democrats who expect to profit from the bill "will use the argument that the Republican party had a majority in the Legislature, and will falsely, but hopefully, charge it

upon Republicans as a partisan crime against the state."

Indeed, all of the southern states, except Mississippi, used state credit to finance the rebuilding and expansion of their railroads, for private sources of credit were inadequate. This policy had been developed before the war; it was continued under the Johnsonians; and in some cases when the Democrats overthrew the radicals there was no decline in the state's generosity to the railroads. While the radicals controlled the southern legislatures, not only they but many members of the Democratic minority as well voted for railroad bond issues. According to an historian of reconstruction in Louisiana, "Such measures were supported by members of both parties, often introduced by Democrats, in every case supported by a large majority of Democrats in both houses."[4] The subservience of many postwar southern legislatures to the demands of railroad and other business promoters is in some respect less shocking than pathetic. For it expressed a kind of blind faith shared by many Southerners of both parties that railroad building and industrialization would swiftly solve all of their section's problems. No price seemed too high for such a miracle.

In several states, for obviously partisan reasons, the actual increase in the size of the public debt was grossly exaggerated. In Mississippi, for example, there was a durable legend among white Democrats that the radicals had added $20,000,000 to the state debt, when, in fact, they added only $500,000. Mississippi radicals had guarded against extravagance by inserting a clause in the

[4] Ella Lonn: *Reconstruction in Louisiana after 1868* (New York, 1918), pp. 36–37.

constitution of 1868 prohibiting the pledging of state funds to aid private corporations—a clause which the conservatives, incidentally, had opposed. In Alabama, apart from railroad bonds secured by railroad property, the radicals added only $2,500,000 to the state debt. They did not leave a debt of $30,000,000 as conservatives claimed. In most other states, when loans to the railroads are subtracted, the increases in state debts for which the radicals were responsible appear far less staggering.

As for taxes, one of the positive achievements of many of the radical governments was the adoption of more equitable tax systems which put a heavier burden upon the planters. Before the war the southern state governments had performed few public services and the tax burden on the landed class had been negligible; hence the vehement protests of the landholders were sometimes as much against radical tax policies as against the alleged waste of taxpayers' money. The restoration governments often brought with them a return to the old inequitable fiscal systems. In Mississippi the subsequent claim of the conservatives that they had reduced the tax burden the radicals had placed upon property holders was quite misleading. The conservatives did lower the state property tax, but, as a consequence, they found it necessary to shift various services and administrative burdens from the state to the counties. This led to an increase in the cost of county government, an increase in the rate of county taxes, and a net increase in total taxes, state and county, that Mississippi property holders had to pay.

As a matter of fact, taxes, government expenditures, and public debts were bound to increase in the southern states during the postwar years no matter who controlled them. For there was no way to escape the staggering job of physical reconstruction—the repair of public buildings, bridges, and roads—and costs had started to go up under the Johnson governments before the radicals came to power. So far from the expenditures of the reconstruction era being totally lost in waste and fraud, much of this physical reconstruction was accomplished while the radicals were in office. They expanded the state railroad systems, increased public services, and provided public school systems—in some states for the first time. Since schools and other public services were now provided for Negroes as well as for whites, a considerable increase in the cost of state government could hardly have been avoided. In Florida between 1869 and 1873 the number of children enrolled in the public schools trebled; in South Carolina between 1868 and 1876 the number increased from 30,000 to 123,000. The economies achieved by some of the restoration governments came at the expense of the schools and various state institutions such as hospitals for the insane. The southern propertied classes had always been reluctant to tax themselves to support education or state hospitals, and in many cases the budget-cutting of the conservatives simply strangled them.

Thus radical rule, in spite of its shortcomings, was by no means synonymous with incompetence and corruption; far too many carpetbagger, scalawag, and Negro politicians made creditable records to warrant such a generalization. Moreover, conditions were improving in the final years of reconstruction. In South Carolina the last radical administration, that of the carpetbagger Governor Daniel H. Chamberlain, was dedicated to reform; in Florida "the financial steadiness of the state government increased toward the end of Republican rule."[5] In Mississippi the radicals made a remarkably good record. The first radical governor, James L. Alcorn, a scalawag, was a man of complete integrity; the second, Adelbert Ames, a carpetbagger, was honest, able, and sincerely devoted to protecting the rights of the Negroes. Mississippi radicals, according to Vernon L. Wharton, established a system of public education far better than any the state had known before; reorganized the state judiciary and adopted a new code of laws; renovated public buildings and constructed new ones, including state hospitals at Natchez and Vicksburg; and provided better state asylums for the blind, deaf, and dumb. The radicals, Wharton concludes, gave Mississippi "a government of greatly expanded functions at a cost that was low in comparison with that of almost any other state."[6] No major political scandal occurred in Mississippi during the years of radical rule—indeed, it was the best governed state in the postwar South. Yet white conservatives attacked the radical regime in Mississippi as violently as they did in South Carolina, which suggests that their basic grievance was not corruption but race policy.

Finally, granting all their mistakes, the radical governments were by far the most democratic the South had ever known. They were the only governments in southern history to extend to Negroes complete civil and political equality, and to try to protect them in the enjoyment of the rights they were granted. The overthrow of these governments was hardly a victory for political democracy, for the conservatives who "redeemed" the South tried to relegate poor men, Negro and white, once more to political obscurity. Near the end of the nineteenth century another battle for political democracy would have to be waged; but this time it would be, for the most part, a more limited version—for whites only. As for the Negroes, they would have to struggle for another century to regain what they had won—and then lost—in the years of radical reconstruction.

[5] William W. Davis: *The Civil War and Reconstruction in Florida* (New York, 1913), pp. 672–673.

[6] [Vernon L.] Wharton, *The Negro in Mississippi* [1865–1890 (Chapel Hill, 1947)] pp. 179–180.

An aspect of historical writing that has concerned many historians is the relationship between a scholar's conclusions and the ideological convictions of his generation. In comparing two works of Dunning and Stampp, THOMAS J. PRESSLY (b. 1919) calls for use of the quantitative approach in solving this dilemma. Professor of history at the University of Washington, he is the author of the highly regarded *Americans Interpret Their Civil War* (1954). While historians have debated the applicability of quantification to their craft, other social scientists have given it enthusiastic support. The student will find that the controversy surrounding the use of quantitative techniques is not restricted to Reconstruction, but has involved the entire span of history.*

▶ *Racial Attitudes, Scholarship, and Reconstruction*

Professor Kenneth M. Stampp's *Era of Reconstruction* is an impressive synthesis and summary of those newer views concerning Reconstruction which, foreshadowed in a few writings published before the Second World War, have increasingly been expressed in the past twenty years, to the point that now they seem to be dominant among the publishing scholars in the field. Since the ideas dominant among the publishing scholars in a field almost invariably become, in one form or another, the ideas dominant in the college and high school textbooks and lecture notes, and then in the minds of a generation or more of students, we are witnessing what is apparently a major shift in the perception and understanding of a crucial era in the history of the United States. Both the change in substantive views of Reconstruction and also the process of shifting perceptions of the past raise issues of the most fundamental nature concerning the enterprise which forms the vocation and avocation of historians, the attempt to understand the past.

The change in substantive views of Reconstruction can be seen concretely by comparing Professor Stampp's book with

* Thomas J. Pressly, "Racial Attitudes, Scholarship and Reconstruction: A Review Essay," *Journal of Southern History*, XXXII (February, 1966), 88–93. Copyright © 1966 by the Southern Historical Association. Reprinted by permission of the Managing Editor. One footnote omitted.

the recently reprinted *Essays on the Civil War and Reconstruction* by William A. Dunning.[1] The first of these seven essays was published in 1886 (when Dunning was twenty-nine years of age), and they were collected in volume form in 1897. A revised edition in 1904 substituted a new concluding essay printed in 1901, and it is this edition which is now reprinted. The Dunning *Essays* occupy a historiographical position somewhat different from Stampp's *Era of Reconstruction*, in that Stampp's volume is a summary of a transformation of ideas which has already taken place among the specialists, a summary based primarily on the findings of scholars other than himself. By contrast, Dunning's essays were among the earliest scholarly expressions of ideas which were later to become widely accepted among historians, and were to become widely accepted in considerable measure through the writing and teaching of Dunning himself. But, despite that difference, it seems accurate to consider Dunning's views as broadly characteristic of many historians from the 1890's to the 1930's and to consider the ideas of Stampp as representative of the perspectives which came into their own among historians of Reconstruction in the 1950's and 1960's.

Reconstruction was described by Dunning in the *Essays* as essentially a racial-political revolution which transferred political power from Southern whites to Negroes. He maintained that Negroes during Radical Reconstruction "exercised an influence in political affairs out

[1] *Essays on the Civil War and Reconstruction.* By William Archibald Dunning. *Harper Torchbook.* (New York: Harper & Row, 1965, Pp. xx, 397. Index. $1.95.)

of all relation to their intelligence or property" (p. 354), and his description of Negroes was not flattering. ". . . the negroes who rose to prominence and leadership" in Reconstruction, ran one of his summations, "were very frequently of a type which acquired and practiced the tricks and knavery rather than the useful arts of politics, and the vicious courses of these negroes strongly confirmed the prejudices of the whites" (p. 355). In a similarly unflattering vein was Dunning's description of those Southern whites who supported the Radical Reconstruction program, the "scalawags" or "loyalists": "a class which lacked the moral authority to conduct government in the Southern states" (pp. 150, 186), individuals who "ran to open disgrace" in "very frequent instances" (p. 355). Any brief and selective summary of an individual's ideas runs the risk of creating an oversimplified and inaccurate impression, and it should be emphasized that Dunning did not express hostility to all aspects of Radical Reconstruction, that he was not an uncritical defender of all Southern "conservative" whites, and that he was not an uncritical defender of the most highly placed opponent of Radical Reconstruction, Andrew Johnson.

Yet, while the qualifications in Dunning's criticism of Radical Reconstruction and its supporters should be noted, his *Essays* make clear his fundamental and pervasive disapproval of what he described as the "seven unwholesome years" of Reconstruction (p. 252). The disapproval seems to have rested ultimately upon Dunning's conviction that Reconstruction as revolution had produced a racial-political order which was both undesirable and unstable, because it sought "to stand the social pyramid on its apex," to "maintain the freedmen . . . on the necks of their former masters" (pp. 250–252). The racial-political revolution of Reconstruction had been justified by individuals whom Dunning called "the emotionalists" (Garrison, Sumner, Phillips, Chase), whose "abstract theories of equality" and "trite generalities of the Rights of Man" had come to be accepted "in the frenzy of the war time" and "during the prevalence of the abolitionist fever" (pp. 251, 384). Fortunately, in Dunning's view, a different group of leaders (Jefferson, Clay, Lincoln) had correctly seen that whites and Negroes were so "distinct in characteristics as to render coalescence impossible . . ." (p. 384). The ideas of this second group had re-emerged in reaction to Radical Reconstruction, leading to the realization that slavery must be replaced "by some set of conditions which, if more humane and beneficent . . . must in essence express the same fact of racial inequality" (p. 384). The *Essays* close with a striking and altogether remarkable passage, first published in 1901, in which Dunning cites the events associated with the overseas expansion of the United States around the turn of the century as confirmation of the concept of racial inequality and as evidence that there would probably never be further attempts to establish racial equality in this country: "In view of the questions which have been raised by our lately established relations with other races, it seems most improbable that the historian will soon, or ever, have to record a reversal of the conditions [of racial inequality] which . . . [the undoing of Reconstruction] has established" (p. 385).

If Dunning found confirmation for his views of Reconstruction in the events of his own day, so, too, does Professor Stampp, although both the events of Professor Stampp's day and his own views of Reconstruction differ markedly from those of Dunning. The noteworthy passage with which Dunning closed his volume of essays is matched by an equally striking passage with which Professor Stampp concludes his volume: "The Fourteenth and Fifteenth Amendments, which could have been adopted only under the conditions of radical reconstruction, make the blunders of that era, tragic though they were, dwindle into insignificance. For if it was worth four years of civil war to save the Union, it was worth a few years of radical reconstruction to give the American Negro the ultimate promise of equal civil and political rights" (p. 215).

To historians who share the relativistic views expressed in some of Carl Becker's essays, the comparison between Dunning and Stampp could seem a characteristic example, in which the shift in the concerns of Mr. Everyman over a period of sixty or seventy years has now been reflected in the shift in the outlook of historians. The issues of Dunning's day ("questions which have been raised by our lately established relations with other races") provided him with a base perspective, which he accepted as axiomatic and from which he confidently disapproved of Radical Reconstruction, while recognizing some virtues in it. In a similar fashion, the issues of Professor Stampp's day ("the ultimate promise of equal civil and political rights" for the American Negro) provide him a base perspective, which he accepts as axiomatic and from which he confidently praises Radical Reconstruction, while recognizing some tragic blunders in it. The "climate of opinion" of Dunning's day had exalted "stability" and practical recognition of racial inequality as desirable touchstones for evaluating Reconstruction, whereas the climate of opinion of Professor Stampp's day exalts as a desirable touchstone for evaluation the ideal of achieving equality between whites and Negroes—and Professor Stampp portrays sympathetically the "idealism" of the Radical Republicans, which he ascribes to "faith" mostly derived from religion (p. 12).

But historians who find unconvincing or unappealing "relativism" of the type expressed by Becker can object that the shift in outlook from Dunning to Stampp should be explained, not in terms of changing "climates of opinion," but in terms of the "progress of historical scholarship." The collecting and sifting of evidence by scholars, it can be maintained, has led historians of today to make descriptive statements of fact which differ from those of Dunning and has thus led to evaluations and interpretations different from those of Dunning. Professor Stampp's descriptive statements are, in actuality, based to a considerable extent upon the findings of scholars since Dunning's era, and Stampp's descriptive statements do differ decidedly from those by Dunning. In contrast, for example, to Dunning's description of Negroes in Reconstruction, Stampp states that Negroes did not control any of the Reconstruction governments and that only a handful reached high office. Of the few Negroes who did occupy high offices in the State governments, "Nearly all . . . were men of ability and integrity" (p. 167). While the mass of Southern Negroes, as portrayed in Stampp's pages, were mostly illiterate, yet they "fully appreciated the importance of achieving literacy, and . . . took advantage of the limited educational opportunities offered them with almost pathetic eagerness" (p. 166). With respect to "scalawags," just as with respect to Negroes, Stampp's descriptions differ from Dunning's. The rather unsavory "scalawags" portrayed by Dunning are replaced in Stampp's volume by a complex group of individuals, some of whom were distinguished leaders of the planter class. A brief and selective summary can distort Stampp's views as much as it can Dunning's, and it should be understood that Stampp depicts some Negroes who were "aggressive," and some Negroes and "scalawags" who were corrupt, although his characterizations as a whole are sympathetic to the two groups.

Whether the changes in outlook from Dunning to Stampp be explained through the "progress of historical scholarship" or through the shifting "climate of opinion" or through some combination of the two factors, it seems likely that Professor Stampp's *Era of Reconstruction* will prove to be an influential statement of the newer views concerning Reconstruction. Its clear, readable, and expert synthesis of the recent scholarship should have appeal for both specialist and nonspecialist readers. Moreover, since the recent scholarship offers intellectual reinforcement and encouragement to opponents of racial discrimination, the volume will speak to the conviction of many individuals in the 1960's.

It is precisely at this point that the example of Dunning raises fundamental and vexing questions. For Dunning also spoke to the convictions of many individuals of his time, and, from the perspective of the newer Reconstruction scholarship, it would seem that he was so wrapped up in the convictions of his time that it affected adversely his scholarship concerning Negroes, "scalawags," and other individuals and topics in Reconstruction. Dunning's presidential address before the American Historical Association in 1913 still stands as a perceptive and understanding discussion of "Truth in History," and, if the Dunning who wrote that address could be misled as scholar by the ideological convictions of his time, warning is served on us all. The warning applies to everyone who tries to understand the past, but in this particular case it is specifically relevant to historians who oppose racial discrimination and who are sympathetic to the newer views of Reconstruction—and I include myself in this group. If Dunning would have been a better historian had he cautioned himself that, since he was convinced of racial inequality, he should check with great care those findings about Negroes and "scalawags" which fitted in so neatly with his belief, should not historians today caution themselves that, since they believe in racial equality, they should examine with particular rigor those findings which coincide with their convictions?

My own view is that more systematic and comprehensive research, using quantitative techniques where feasible and relevant to supplement traditional methods, would help historians guard against potential distortions in understanding the past arising from their own ideological convictions. Until such methods are used, those who share Dunning's views can cite Negroes and "scalawags" who were corrupt and incompetent, while those who favor the newer views can cite examples to the contrary—each group using the same technique of "proof by selective quotation," although holding different ideologies. But, whatever the methods used by historians, the example of Dunning stands as reminder that the passage of time and the shifting of beliefs can starkly reveal the extent to which scholarship rests upon durable evidence and the extent to which it rests upon ideological convictions. What will be the verdict of historians fifty years hence concerning the newer views of Reconstruction?

While many historians reject an economic interpretation of Reconstruction, very few exclude the importance of economics. JAMES M. McPHERSON (b. 1936) of Princeton University has devoted two books, *The Struggle for Equality* (1964) and *The Negro's Civil War* (1965), and a number of articles to white attitudes toward the Negro as well as Negro history. In the following excerpt from one of these studies, he advances the argument that the failure to provide the freedmen with land left them in an insecure position following Reconstruction. His reasons for the shortcomings of the era offer an interesting dissent from those of Dunning.*

▶ # The Failure to Achieve Land Reform

Abolitionist efforts to win suffrage and education for the freedmen were partially successful. The same cannot be said of their attempts to obtain land for the emancipated Negroes. After the war many abolitionists stepped up their agitation for the confiscation and redistribution of large plantations. "The nominal freedom of the slaves . . . must be actually secured by the possession of land," wrote Edmund Quincy in April 1865. "If the monopoly of land be permitted to remain in the hands of the present rebel proprietors . . . the monopoly of labor might almost as well be given them, too." Wendell Phillips, Anna Dickinson, Gerrit Smith, Lydia Maria Child, James Freeman Clarke, Thomas Wentworth Higginson, and many other abolitionists echoed these sentiments.

President Johnson's amnesty proclamation of May 29, 1865, dealt a sharp blow to radicals who hoped for wholesale confiscation. The proclamation restored political and property rights to most rebels who would take an oath of allegiance. In subsequent months Johnson issued a large number of special pardons to men who had been exempted

* From James M. McPherson, *The Struggle for Equality: Abolitionists and the Negro in the Civil War and Reconstruction.* Reprinted by permission of the Princeton University Press. Copyright © 1964 by the Princeton University Press. Pp. 407–416. Footnotes omitted.

from the May 29 proclamation. Despite this setback, abolitionists continued to work for governmental action to secure land for the freedmen. They hoped for congressional reversal of Johnson's policy of property restoration, just as they hoped for congressional reversal of the rest of his reconstruction program. Several radical Republican leaders agreed with the abolitionists on this question. "We must see that the freedmen are established on the soil, and that they may become proprietors," wrote Charles Sumner. "From the beginning I have regarded confiscation only as ancillary to emancipation." In his famous speech at Lancaster, Pennsylvania, on September 6, 1865, Thaddeus Stevens advocated confiscation of the property of large southern landholders and the grant of 40 acres to each adult freedman. But most Republicans shied away from the radicalism of wholesale confiscation. Prospects for the adoption of Stevens' proposal or anything like it appeared dim in 1865.

One of the anticipated functions of the Freedmen's Bureau was resettlement of freedmen on abandoned and confiscated land. Johnson's pardon and amnesty program, however, threatened to leave the Bureau with very little land for this purpose. In August 1865, Johnson issued a series of executive orders to General Howard[1] instructing him to restore all confiscated property to former rebel owners except that which had already been sold under court decrees. These orders affected nearly all lands under Bureau control. The status of property along the South Atlantic coast assigned to the freedmen by Sherman's

[1] Oliver O. Howard was commissioner of the Freedmen's Bureau.—Ed.

Order no. 15 . . . became a burning issue during the winter of 1865–1866. More than 40,000 freedmen lived on 485,000 acres with the "possessory titles" granted by Sherman's Order. In October 1865, Johnson sent General Howard to the sea islands to persuade the freedmen to return their farms to the pardoned owners. Howard had no taste for his mission, but like a good soldier he carried out his superior's orders. He urged the freedmen quietly to abandon their farms and go back to work for their former masters.

Freedmen on the sea islands could hardly believe their ears. "To turn us off from the land that the Government has allowed us to occupy, is nothing less than returning us to involuntary servitude," said one of them. "They will make freedom a curse to us, for we have no home, no land, no oath, no vote, and consequently no country." Some of the Negroes vowed to defend their farms by force if necessary. Abolitionists summoned all their eloquence to denounce the government's action. "This villainous effort to rob loyal men for the benefit of ruffianly rebels whose hands are red with the blood of Northern soldiers, can succeed only through a breach of faith on the part of our government such as would be without parallel in history," declared the *Commonwealth*. The *Right Way* asked: "Shall our own, and all coming ages, brand us for the treachery of sacrificing our faithful friends to our and their enemies? GOD IN HIS MERCY SAVE US FROM SUCH PERFIDY AND SUCH IDIOCY." General Rufus Saxton, commissioner of the Freedmen's Bureau in South Carolina, refused to carry out the order dispossessing the Negroes of their land, and Johnson removed Saxton from office on

January 15, 1866. Even after Saxton's removal the Freedmen's Bureau moved slowly, hoping that Congress would enact legislation nullifying the president's orders.

In the end most of the freedmen were dispossessed. But the Freedmen's Bureau bill passed over Johnson's veto in July 1866, contained a provision for the lease of 20 acres of government-owned land on the sea islands to each dispossessed freedman with a six-year option to buy at $1.50 per acre. At the same time Congress passed the Southern Homestead Act, extending the principle of the homestead law of 1862 to the public lands of Alabama, Arkansas, Florida, Louisiana, and Mississippi. The bill stipulated that until January 1, 1867, no one who had supported the Confederacy would be eligible for a homestead. This provision was intended to give the freedmen and Unionist whites first chance at the land. Abolitionists hoped for good results from the Southern Homestead Act, but their hopes were doomed to disappointment. Most of the lands opened for settlement were of inferior quality, and few freedmen had the necessary capital to buy tools and farm implements or to support themselves while they were trying to coax the first crop from the sandy soil. As a means of placing the freedmen on fertile land of their own, the Southern Homestead Act was a failure.

Abolitionists soon discerned the inadequacy of the Homestead Act and renewed their demands for a program of confiscation and redistribution of southern plantations. An abolitionist traveler in the South reported in the fall of 1866 that the destitution of landless freedmen was appalling. He was alarmed by the nascent share-cropping and crop-lien systems that were taking root in the South. The Negroes "appear to have neither mind nor hope above their present condition, and will continue to work on from day to day, and from year to year, without more than enough to keep soul and body together," wrote the traveler. "When addressing their masters, they take off their hats, and speak in a hesitating, trembling manner, as though they were in the presence of a Superior Being." The freedman could never improve his status as long as he remained landless and penniless. "No other government ever ended a great rebellion before without confiscating the estates of principal rebels, and placing that mighty power, the landed interest, on its side."

In the spring of 1867 abolitionists stepped up their agitation for confiscation, hoping to win public support for such a policy before the next session of Congress. The *Boston Commonwealth* published a series of militant editorials, some of them by Elizur Wright, calling for expropriation. Wright chided "practical" Republican politicians who shrank from the radicalism of confiscation: "O ye mighty 'practical' men! don't you know—are you not sensible—does it not ever enter your noddles to suspect —that if you have thirty thousand disloyal nabobs to own more than half the land of the South, they, and nobody else, will *be* the South? That they laugh, now in their sleeves, and by-and-bye will laugh out of their sleeves, at your schoolma'ams and ballot-boxes? *They who own the real estate of a country control its vote.*"

At the annual meeting of the American Anti-Slavery Society in May 1867, Phillips introduced a resolution urging agrarian reform in the South as "an act of justice" to the Negro. Several speakers supported the resolution. Higginson said that confiscation "is an essential part of abolition. To give to these people only freedom, without the land, is to give them only the mockery of freedom which the English or the Irish peasant has." Without land the Negro voter would be at the mercy of the planter, who could use economic coercion to dictate his vote. "The time will come," said Higginson, "when the nation must recognize that even political power does not confer safety upon a race of landless men." Phillips' resolution was adopted almost unanimously by the Society. The New England Anti-Slavery Society passed a similar resolution three weeks later. In the following months Phillips hammered away relentlessly at the confiscation theme. "What we want to give the negro is what the masses must have or they are practically serfs, the world over," he declared. Confiscation during the French Revolution crippled the aristocracy; confiscation uprooted Toryism in the American Revolution. "Land is the usual basis of government," said Phillips; "the class that hold it must, in the long run, give tone and character to the Administration. It is manifestly suicidal, therefore, to leave it in the hands of the hostile party."

But abolitionists were fighting a losing battle on the confiscation front. A majority of the Republican party was opposed to the measure. The *New York Times* thought that "the colored race is likely to be injured, rather than aided, by this sycophantic and extravagant crusade on its behalf." The *Times* urged friends of the freedmen to teach the lessons of labor, patience, frugality, and virtue to the Negro rather than demand special favors for him. Horace Greeley

thought the agitation for confiscation was "either knavery or madness. People who want farms work for them. The only class we know that takes other people's property because they want it is largely represented in Sing Sing." The Democratic gains in the 1867 elections put a virtual end to the drive for confiscation. The mood of radicalism which might have sustained confiscation in 1866 or 1867 had passed away. There was no longer any chance (if indeed there ever had been) that Congress would pass a confiscation bill or any other wholesale measure to provide farms for the freedmen.

In 1869 abolitionists set forth a new plan to obtain land for the freedmen. Aaron M. Powell, editor of the *Anti-Slavery Standard*, drew up a petition urging Congress to create a federal land commission, to be composed of "well-known, disinterested friends of the freed people." The commission would be capitalized at $2,000,000 by the U.S. Treasury and empowered to buy up large tracts of available southern land for resale in small lots to the freedmen at low cost and on easy terms. The commission would also be authorized to make loans to the freedmen for transportation, tools, implements, building materials, and seed. Abolitionists circulated the petition widely in 1869–1870, obtaining thousands of signatures from southern freedmen as well as their northern sympathizers. A Tennessee congressman introduced a bill to create such a land commission, but it died in committee, the last monument to Congress's failure to place the freedmen in a position of economic viability.

Abolitionists backed several private schemes to settle the freedmen on farms of their own. In 1865 a group of Boston and New York capitalists incorporated the "American Land Company and Agency," with Governor John Andrew as president. George L. Stearns was one of the largest stockholders in this company, whose purpose was to channel northern investment into the South to help rebuild the section's economy and settle as many freedmen as possible on land of their own. Andrew and Stearns reasoned that the war had left southern planters poor in everything except land. They planned to buy part of this land in order to provide the planters with enough capital to farm the remainder. The company could then resell some of its purchased property to the freedmen. Things went badly from the beginning, however. The company invested heavily in Tennessee cotton plantations, but crop failures in 1866 ate up most of the capital. Stearns' death in the spring of 1867 brought the enterprise to bankruptcy and failure.

Not all of the private efforts to provide freedmen with land were failures. In 1865 John G. Fee, a Kentucky-born abolitionist and cofounder of Berea College, purchased 130 acres in central Kentucky and resold the land in small tracts to freedmen, who established a village on the property. In 1891 there were 42 families living in this village. Fee urged the American Missionary Association to go into the business of selling land to the freedmen. In 1868 the A.M.A. began purchasing plantations for resale to Negroes. On each tract of land the A.M.A. established a church and school, and several small agricultural villages grew up in the South around these A.M.A. centers. The A.F.U.C.[2] also had a small fund for the purchase and resale of

[2] American Freedmen's Union Commission.— Ed.

farms to the freedmen. In 1869 a group of Boston abolitionists and philanthropists purchased a plantation in Georgia and started a "Southern Industrial School and Labor Enterprise." William and Ellen Craft, a couple who had escaped from slavery before the war, went to Georgia to manage the enterprise. They were accompanied by Yankee farmers who taught the freedmen the latest methods of planting, seeding, plowing, and so on. The freedmen attended the vocational and agricultural school part of the day and worked in the fields the rest of the time. They were encouraged to save their wages to buy land for themselves. The Ku Klux Klan burned the crop and buildings of the plantation in 1871, but the Crafts rebuilt the school and carried on in Georgia until 1878, when they sold the plantation in small tracts to the freedmen and returned to Boston.

One of the most ambitious abolitionist efforts to secure land for the freedmen by private investment was a plan developed by Charles Stearns, an old-line Garrisonian from Springfield, Massachusetts. In 1854 Stearns had gone to Kansas to fight for freedom, and in 1860 he drifted west to Colorado Territory. He went to Georgia in May 1866, and purchased a 1,500-acre plantation near Augusta. He hoped to run the plantation for a few years on the cooperative principle and then sell it in small tracts to the freedmen who had worked for him.

Stearns was filled with enthusiasm for his project when he first came South. He established night and Sunday schools to teach his laborers to read and write. Southern neighbors told him that he could never "manage the niggers" with kindness, but would be compelled to use force and punishment if he wanted to get any work out of them. Stearns hoped to prove his neighbors wrong. He substituted kindness, incentive bonuses, and moral suasion for insults and punishment. In a summary of his experiences written several years later, Stearns admitted that the practical realities of the situation had soon modified his enthusiasm. The freedmen were inefficient workers and destroyed tools and implements by their carelessness. Stearns almost succumbed to disillusionment and despair several times. But he always rallied himself with the thought that slavery was a poor school for efficiency, honesty, or skill, and returned to work with renewed dedication. He later evaluated his experiment as a success. After six years the Negroes on his plantation were better educated, more honest, and more industrious than when he first came.

Inability to pay off the mortgage on his plantation forced Stearns to postpone his plans to sell the land to his employees. In 1869 his creditors threatened to foreclose, and Stearns hurried to Boston to raise $6,000 to pay the mortgage. Samuel Sewall and Wendell Phillips listened sympathetically to Stearns' proposition. Sewall gave him a $1,000 loan, and Phillips and Sewall helped him raise the remaining $5,000. He returned to Georgia and inaugurated his plan to sell the plantation in 25-acre lots to the Negroes. Only 20 freedmen were able to buy during the first year, and some of them soon fell behind on their payments. By the end of 1870 Stearns was in debt again and about ready to give up in despair. "I am certain I can never cultivate a farm successfully with the blacks as laborers," he wrote in his diary.

"Nothing can be done without incessant and minute supervision of them, such as I am not able to give." He almost sold the plantation to one of his white neighbors, but his mother, who had come South to teach the freedmen, convinced him that to do so would be a breach of faith with the Negroes he had worked so hard to help. Stearns heeded her pleas. He stayed on for another year and began writing a book about his experiences in an effort to promote northern interest in the needs of the freedmen.

In 1872 Stearns brought a group of 50 Massachusetts farmers and missionaries to his plantation to establish an agricultural and industrial colony. The Yankee farmers soon transformed the establishment into a model of efficiency and neatness. Most of the Negroes stayed on the plantation and tried to learn better methods of farming from the Yankees. Stearns returned to Boston to finish his book and to set on foot a project for northern purchase and resale of southern plantations to freedmen. In 1873 he organized a "Laborers' Homestead and Southern Emigration Society" with a planned capitalization of $50,000. Samuel Gridley Howe served as president, and Stearns, Phillips, and James Buffum (an abolitionist) acted as a three-man board of trustees. The Society purchased some property in Virginia to start their experiment. Stearns sent out hundreds of circulars urging capitalists to invest in his Society. Lands purchased by the trustees would be resold in 25-acre tracts on easy terms to freedmen and northern settlers. The Society planned also to make loans to the purchasers to enable them to buy tools, seed, and implements. Stearns had grandiose plans for his Society. He urged Congress to lend it $1,000,000 per year for ten years. Congress took no note of his appeal, however, and the panic of 1873 soon dried up Stearns' meager sources of private capital. Apart from the Georgia plantation and the property in Virginia he had little to show for his efforts. He had established one agricultural colony and sold land to several dozen freedmen. It was a rather small ending to an ambitious beginning.

In 1880 Frederick Douglass attributed the failure of Reconstruction to the refusal of Congress to provide the freedmen with an opportunity to obtain good land of their own. "Could the nation have been induced to listen to those stalwart Republicans, Thaddeus Stevens and Charles Sumner, some of the evils which we now suffer would have been averted," declared Douglass. "The negro would not today be on his knees, as he is, supplicating the old master class to give him leave to toil. . . . He would not now be swindled out of his hard earnings by money orders for wages with no money in them." Many abolitionists still alive in 1880 would have agreed with Douglass. They had done their best to call attention to the necessity of land for the freedmen, but the nation was not sympathetic enough toward the plight of the Negro to provide any adequate means by which he could obtain land. As a result the Negroes remained economically a subordinate class, dependent upon white landowners or employers for their livelihood. The South was not "reconstructed" economically, and consequently the other measures of reconstruction rested upon an unstable foundation.

The English-trained historian W. R. BROCK (b. 1916), who has taught in England as well as the United States, has written two major studies of American life: *The Character of American History* (1960) and *An American Crisis: Congress and Reconstruction, 1865–1867*. In the latter work he advances the concept: when in the racial ideology of a majority a minority is considered to be its inferior, positive legal safeguards are needed to protect the minority. Brock believes this is particularly important for Reconstruction because such Radicals as Thaddeus Stevens and Charles Sumner held views on Negro equality that ran counter to the thinking of most Americans. It is against this background that he evaluates Radical Reconstruction.*

Racial Ideology and the Weaknesses of Radical Reconstruction

It has been argued that much of the Radical success was explained by the pressures from below which drove cautious politicians even further than they had intended, and that this pressure must be explained in ideological terms and not as the product of mere interest groups. The ideology had expressed in abstract but attractive terms certain propositions about man in society which, for a moment in time, seemed to epitomise the aspirations of the Northern people. Racial equality, equal rights and the use of national authority to secure both were living ideas in the Reconstruc-tion era as they have since become, in some quarters, in the mid-twentieth century. For the first time these concepts were cast in the form of a political pro-gramme which could be achieved; but their success depended upon the response which they aroused from the Northern people. After Reconstruction the ideas persisted but failed to rouse the same enthusiasm; their formal acceptance was a very different thing from the popular emotion which could push them for-ward despite the usual obstacles to policies which disturb complacency and refuse to let men rest in peace. The ques-

* From W. R. Brock, *An American Crisis: Congress and Reconstruction, 1865–1867* (New York: St. Martin's Press, 1963), pp. 284–303. Reprinted by permission of St. Martin's Press, Inc., Macmillan & Co., Ltd. Footnotes omitted.

tion remains whether the slackening of the pressure behind the Radical ideology should be explained by rival distractions and changing interests or by a weakness in the ideology itself. Examination will show that the generalities of the Radical ideology—so attractive at first sight—could not stand pressure. The weapons bent and broke in the hands of those who used them.

A belief in racial equality has never won universal assent and to the majority of men in the mid-nineteenth century it seemed to be condemned both by experience and by science. The literal equality between men of obviously different physiological characteristics was an abolitionist invention and it rested upon emotional conviction rather than upon rational proof; the comparison between intelligent negroes and retarded poor whites proved little because the civilization of a few blacks did not redeem the mass from docile ignorance and the degradation of some whites did not detract from the high standards of the majority. The abolitionist argument was based largely upon pure *a priori* statements or upon experience with fugitive slaves; a mass of argument could be produced against the one, while the defiance of the occasional runaway did not prove that the mass of his fellows were not fitted by nature for a subordinate position. The behaviour of the negro was obviously different from that of the whites and, though those who knew him best granted him some admirable traits, they would also maintain that he was sadly deficient in the capacity for industry, thrift, self-reliance, enterprise, sexual restraint and the whole galaxy of virtues esteemed by nineteenth-century civilization. The abolitionist argu-

ment that the negro appeared "inferior" because he had lived in slavery for generations failed to carry weight because no free negro society could be found to prove the proposition. Moreover there was an added complication in the mixed ancestry of so many of those who, like Frederick Douglass, were quoted as evidence of innate negro intelligence. This is not the place to enter upon the tangled problem of racial characteristics; it is sufficient to state that in the later nineteenth century racial equality was a hypothesis which was generally rejected. It was not accepted in the North any more than it was in the South and even abolitionists were anxious to disclaim any intention of forcing social contacts between the races and all shied away from the dread subject of racial amalgamation. An initial weakness of the Radical ideology was therefore its dependence upon a concept which was not self-evident, lacked scientific proof, and offended popular susceptibilities.

The usual weakness of equalitarian theory lies in demonstrating that people ought to be treated as equals in spite of natural inequalities, and this difficulty is acute when dealing with people of different races. While it is possible to argue, among men of the same race, that it is necessary to treat men as though they were equal, it is far harder to do so in the face of popular prejudice that men of a different race are marked at birth as "inferior." The conventional Republican argument was that men were unequal in capabilities but equal in rights, and in the American context this proposition rested mainly upon an appeal to the preamble of the Declaration of Independence; but the assertions of the Declaration were not "self-evident" to most white Americans when applied to negroes. Moreover there were some particular difficulties in equalitarian theory when applied to a mass of people, concentrated in a single region, and occupying from time out of mind a subordinate position in society. Equality demands protection of the weak against the strong and positive law to afford it; but it usually involves the assumption that given certain legal rights the due process of law will enable men to maintain their equality. With the negroes this assumption could not be made: what was required was protection, maintained by enforceable law, at every point where the power of the dominant race was likely to impinge upon the weaker. With tradition, economic power, prejudice, social custom and, in most Southern districts, numbers all entrenched on one side, protection could not be provided merely by changing the law and leaving its administration to the local authorities and courts. The concept of negro equality demanded interference with the processes of local government on a scale never before contemplated in America or in any other nation. Would the Northern majority be prepared to exert continuously this kind of pressure and provide this kind of protection? In the answer to this question lay the second great weakness of the Radical ideology.

Further difficulties lay in the complexities which sheltered behind the simple word "equality." Whatever the moral arguments the negro was not, and could not be in the immediate future, an equal to the white man in economic life, in competition for the scarce educational facilities of the South, or in winning public office. Racial equality would have to be an artificial creation imposed upon Southern society; the negro would have to have guarantees which were not given to the white man, and the quest for equality would demand unequal incidence of the law. No other minority required special legislation to ensure equal status in the courts, or the care of a Federal bureau, or the use of force to protect the right to vote. Negro equality implied that something must be taken from the whites, and this was explicit in two features of Radical policy: confiscation and disqualification. Stevens never wavered in his belief that negro democracy must have an economic basis in negro landownership; confiscation and redistribution were therefore cardinal points in his programme. Yet the most passionate advocates of equality could not persuade the Republican majority to embark upon such a disturbance of property. Negro democracy would also be a sham if the former ruling class retained its grasp upon local and national office, and disqualification was necessary. This policy succeeded because it was supported by Northern fear of restored Southern domination at Washington, but it proved to be the most vulnerable and perhaps the least wise aspect of Reconstruction. Both confiscation and disqualification demonstrate the formidable difficulties which attend the imposition of equality upon a society in which it did not exist, and in which the beneficiaries of equalitarian policy were too weak, socially and economically, to stand upon their own feet. The price of equality was revolutionary change, vigilance and constant pressure, and who would pay the price when enthusiasm grew cold and the suspicion grew that the negroes were not yet ready to exercise rights which could not be secured without the coercion of their fellow citizens.

It is in this context that the work of John A. Bingham assumes great significance. In his fight for the civil rights clause of the Fourteenth Amendment he cut equal rights free from negro protection and made them national. The later perversion of this clause to protect the rights of corporations tended to obscure the significance of a measure which protected all citizens and all persons under the jurisdiction of the States, but once the importance of nationalized right was recognized the Fourteenth Amendment grew in stature. Conversely the Fifteenth Amendment was weak from the outset because it linked suffrage with race; it was a law for negro enfranchisement and could be enforced only so long as some people had an interest in doing so. If the Fifteenth Amendment had declared in unequivocal terms that all males over the age of twenty-one who were citizens of the United States had the right to vote it might have been recognized as a cornerstone of democracy and attracted popular support. As it was the Fifteenth Amendment enacted "impartial" suffrage which meant that the States could impose any qualification they chose provided that it was not based on race; this meant that the white majority of the nation had no particular interest in its enforcement.

Beyond the major problem of equality by enforcement lay the vast and ramifying difficulty of definition. Was equality indivisible or if divisible which aspects were essential? The three classic definitions of equality—*in* the eyes of God, *under* the law, and *of* opportunity —each carried different implications.

Equality in the eyes of God might well be an excuse for inequality on earth: Dives and Lazarus had both lived under the judgment of God, both received their deserts after death, and their inequality on earth was dramatic but irrelevant to their condition in eternity. Equality in the eyes of God implied some limitation upon the principle of subordination for it had been an essential part of the abolitionist case that the children of God should not be treated as less than human beings, but it provided no definition of the place of man in society. Many pious Northerners saw no inconsistency between Christian conviction and racial discrimination, and the brotherhood of man in Christ was no barrier to the belief that equality on earth was no part of God's purpose. It was therefore necessary to supplement the Christian concept of equality in eternity with the purely secular arguments for equality on earth.

Equality under the law had deep roots in the Anglo-Saxon tradition but in its mother country it had not proved incompatible with aristocratic privilege, an established Church, denial of suffrage to the masses, and the exploitation of low paid labour. The guarantee of equal status in the courts was a great and important addition to the rights of negroes, but it would not of itself create a political and social revolution. Beyond the formal guarantee of equality under the law lay the intractable question of who should administer the law. The legal rights of negroes might be recognized in Southern courts but they were likely to be strictly interpreted; one could be confident that the white Southern judge would administer the law scrupulously, but between the negro and equal justice stood the white Southern jury. Equality under the law was a grand sweeping theory, without which no other form of secular equality was possible, but it did not erase the notion that the negro was an inferior man to whom only a grudging recognition was extended. It might be argued that, once the groundwork of legal equality had been laid, the progress towards equality in other fields would follow, yet one might doubt the certainty of this hypothesis. It was only in 1867 that the British Parliament was to decide after centuries of equality under the law that the agricultural labourer was entitled to a vote, and millions of simple Englishmen still went unlettered to their graves.

Equality of opportunity seemed to be a more positive demand. If the racial barrier could be removed from access to education, occupation and public office the negro would have the right to compete on equal terms with the whites in most of the fields to which his aspiration might lead him. Yet equality of opportunity implied inequality of achievement and in the South its immediate result might be the confirmation of white supremacy. If the negro was to be given a real chance of equal achievement he must be given positive aids which were not given to the white man, and one was brought back once more to the basic problem of equalitarian theory: that positive government was required to corrupt habitual inequality. This led on to the political difficulty that, in the climate of nineteenth-century opinion, sustained and purposeful government intervention was unpopular and improbable. The comparatively modest aims of the Freedmen's Bureau aroused intense hostility in the South and many doubts in the North; any further attempt to translate the commitment to equality into governmental responsibilities might wreck the whole structure of Reconstruction, yet without this the purpose of equalitarian Radicalism could not be achieved.

Many Republicans contended that it was unnecessary to embark upon the troubled sea of racial equality if one could stop in the safe haven of guaranteed rights. The negro was a man, and as a man he had certain inalienable rights; if these could be secured the vexed question of equality could be deferred or perhaps dismissed. This theory of inalienable right had better prospects than any theory of equality. American tradition had long accepted as its cornerstone the idea of man as an atom in society, entitled to do all that was within his power provided that it did not impinge upon the rights of others. But American tradition had usually failed to recognize the fact that rights were not "inalienable," that the exercise of legal rights depended upon the consent of the majority, or that some rights of some men could always be denied by the sovereign power of the people. In Reconstruction Americans were brought face to face with the problem of free men whose "rights" were denied by the local majority and could be secured only by external coercion. Moreover the whole attitude of Americans towards rights had been governed by their implicit acceptance of the idea of checks and balances. The rights of the people were a check upon the enlargement of authority, and to give some rights to some people at the expense of others had been damned by association with the idea of privilege. What was the intrinsic difference between rights conferred upon a chartered monopoly and rights conferred upon a weak minority? This conundrum had always been implicit in American political discourse but Reconstruction made it explicit.

Even if these pitfalls could be avoided there remained the knotty problem of which rights should be protected and how they could be distinguished from rights which were unprotected. The Declaration of Independence referred to the rights of life, liberty and the pursuit of happiness, but these were *among* the inalienable rights and not an exclusive list; and even if one stopped short at the classic three the pursuit of happiness was so elastic an idea that it was little guide to an enumeration of rights which could be protected by law. There were three main attempts to distinguish the categories of right and to determine which could, and which could not be protected. The first was the distinction between civil rights and political rights, the second between those which were fundamental and those which could be left to the discretion of political authorities, and the third was that between public and private rights. The first proposal made by Thaddeus Stevens— that all laws, state and national, should apply equally to all persons—attempted to cut through this maze of difficulties. Later Sumner was to express the same idea when he said "Show me . . . a legal institution, anything created or regulated by law, and I will show you what must be opened equally to all without distinction of color." This was the true Radical argument. It recognized that private prejudice could not be legislated out of existence, but maintained that discrimination could be prohibited in every activity touched by the law. Stevens and Sumner would have left people to do what they liked in their homes

or in private associations, but they would have outlawed discrimination at the polls, in public places, on public transport, and in education. Sumner even hoped to add churches, cemeteries and benevolent institutions to this list. He resisted the argument of "separate but equal" by asserting that "Equality is where all men are alike. A substitute can never take the place of equality." At the other end of the Republican spectrum was Lyman Trumbull who said the "civil rights" (which should be guaranteed by law) were "the right to his liberty, to come and go as he pleases, have the avails of his own labor, and not to be restricted in that respect." In other respects the legal rights of negroes must depend upon the discretion of their political sovereign for these were "all matters of privilege." This attempted to treat the negro as a free man without treating him as an equal man, and Trumbull even regarded the right to serve on a jury as one of these matters of privilege.

Before the Reconstruction controversy ended moderate Republicans including Trumbull himself, had moved significantly nearer to the Radical view of rights which ought to be guaranteed, but there remained a distinct cleavage between those who believed that wherever the law flowed it should carry with it equality of right, and those who believed that one soon reached a frontier at which a "right" became a "privilege" and could be withheld at the discretion of the legal sovereign. The extreme Radical position was unequivocal and relatively uncomplicated, but would require a large invasion of the traditional areas of State authority; the "moderate" position was clouded with difficulties of definition and separation but in the nature of things it was more likely to appeal to the majority of men who disliked sweeping logic and preferred to believe that the minimum of effort would produce the best results. Under the circumstances the best which the Radicals could obtain was probably the imprecise but traditional phrases which Bingham wrote into the Fourteenth Amendment. The "privileges and immunities" of citizens of the United States, "the equal protection of the laws," and "due process of law" were all expressions which could mean as much or as little as lawyers were prepared to read into them. They did not prevent the Supreme Court from legalizing segregation but they also provided ammunition for the Court's later attack upon segregation. It is possible that Bingham's first suggestion, which would have given to Congress the responsibility for initiating measures to protect rights, would have obviated some of the difficulties inherent in judicial legislation; but Congress, even more than the Court, would be unwilling to act until there was sufficient public interest to support action. Once the Northern majority had refused to accept the principle that wherever the law operated race must be forgotten, and had accepted the distinctions between rights which were rights and rights which were privileges, the whole idea of equality under the law was lost. Natural right became neither more nor less than the right which the majority was prepared to recognize and to protect.

Charles Sumner realized the dangers inherent in the attempt to split up the rights of man into various categories, and devoted the closing years of his life to a struggle for a measure which would have embodied the Stevens principle of equal incidence of national and State laws on all citizens. When he was accused of occupying the time of the Senate with arguments over access to hotel rooms or the exclusion of negroes from benevolent institutions he replied that "Every question by which the equal rights of all are affected is transcendant. It cannot be magnified, But here are the rights of a whole race, not merely the rights of an individual, not merely the rights of two or three or four, but the rights of a whole race." A year after Sumner's death Congress enacted some of the provisions of the bill for which he had fought and guaranteed to the negroes equal rights in hotels, places of public entertainment, and public transport, but did nothing about education. In 1883 the Supreme Court found this Act invalid on the ground that it was intended to protect "social" and not "civil" or "political" rights. In 1896 the Supreme Court upheld a State law requiring segregated facilities on railroads, and the tide of Radicalism which had once lashed so furiously against the ramparts was at its lowest ebb. Only a bold man could have predicted that the stone which the builders rejected was to become a cornerstone of liberal orthodoxy in the second half of the twentieth century.

The Radical solution to the dilemma of rights which were natural but which could only be secured by artificial means was negro suffrage. With the vote the negro would be equipped to protect his own rights, and there were Jeffersonian echoes in the idea that the cultivator of the soil would not only defend his personal rights but also act as a repository for political virtue. The voting negro would protect himself against injustice and the Union against its enemies, but this concept of suffrage as a protective device proved inadequate when Reconstruction governments were compelled to assume the tasks of modern administration in a region where the best government had always been that which governed least. So long as the vote was merely protective the ignorance of the negro was not a relevant argument because a poor man could understand what had to be defended as well as the best educated; but when negro suffrage became the basis for an economic and social revolution guided by positive government it was relevant to ask whether the former slave was yet equal to his responsibilities.

The Radicals argued the case for negro suffrage in the context of nineteenth-century liberal thought, and they can hardly be blamed for not having transcended the ideas of their age. Moreover they were inhibited by the political circumstances in which they had to operate. It was hard enough to convince Northern public opinion that negro suffrage was safe and just without complicating the question. In the summer of 1866 a Radical member of the Reconstruction Committee told Congress that "we may as well state it plainly and fairly, so that there shall be no misunderstanding on the subject. It was our opinion that three fourths of the States of this Union (that is of the loyal States) could not be induced to vote to grant the right of suffrage, even in any degree or under any restriction, to the colored race." Between this time and the passage of the Fifteenth Amendment a remarkable change took place in public opinion, but in order to foster it the Radicals were forced to rely less and less upon appeals

to abstract justice and more and more upon the utility of the negro vote to the party and to the Union. This stress led them to pass lightly over the tasks which negro democracy might be called upon to perform, and to treat their votes merely as a counterweight in the political balance of the nation.

Radicals themselves hesitated at times over the problem of the vote. Was it one of the inalienable rights, or was it, as everyone else said, a political right which could be granted or withheld at the discretion of the political sovereign? Among the conservative Republicans, and particularly amongst the better educated, there was genuine hesitation about mass democracy, and if they turned one eye towards the negroes of the South they turned the other to the foreign-born city vote which formed the electoral basis of Boss Tweed's New York ring. Reformers could join hands with the merely fearful in urging the case for universal literacy tests, and old Know-Nothings could make common cause with new Republicans against universal suffrage. Yet literacy tests which would exclude the mass of the Southern negro people, and could be manipulated by the ruling State authorities, were useless as a political solution in the South, and Radicals were pushed from their early caution on the suffrage question to an outright avowal of belief in universal suffrage. In a letter written for communication to a Republican meeting in New York in January 1868 Thaddeus Stevens insisted that the right to vote was inalienable, and put natural right ahead of the argument from utility, but he went on to stress the other arguments in favour of universal suffrage. "True, I deemed the hastening of the bestowal of that franchise as very essential to the welfare of the nation, because without it I believe that the Government will pass into the hands of the loco-focos, and that such an event will be disastrous to the whole country. With universal suffrage I believe the true men of the nation can maintain their position. Without it whether their suffrage be impartial or qualified I look upon the Republic as likely to relapse into an oligarchy which will be ruled by coarse Copperheadism and proud Conservatism. I have never insisted that the franchise should be unjustly regulated so as to secure a Republican ascendancy but I have insisted and do insist that there can be no unjust regulation of that franchise which will give to any other party the power if the Republicans are true to themselves and do not fall into their usual vice of cowardice. The Republicans once beaten into a minority by the force of Negro prejudice will never again obtain the majority and the nation will become a despotism." Six months before his death Stevens explained that after long reflection he had "finally come to the conclusion that universal suffrage was one of the inalienable rights intended to be inserted in (the Declaration of Independence) by our Fathers at the time of the Revolution and that they were prevented from inserting it in the Constitution by slavery alone." His reflection owed more to the exigencies of contemporary politics than to a knowledge of history, but there is no need to doubt the sincerity of his conclusion. Universal suffrage was the logical and complete answer; "impartial" suffrage was not. With Stevens dead, however, there was no one with the same influence who could put the case so clearly and the

Fifteenth Amendment enacted impartial and not universal suffrage. The Radicals failed in the first instance because they did not or could not spell out what negro democracy was to do, and the second instance because they could not resist the modification of the right to vote which let in literacy tests, grandfather clauses, and poll taxes.

Paradoxically some of the Radical arguments for negro suffrage tended to rebound. The idea that the vote would enable the negro to protect himself provided an excuse for non-intervention, and for the belief that the Southern question could now be treated as a local question. In 1880 James G. Blaine, writing in the *North American Review*, justified the grant of negro suffrage by saying that "had the franchise not been bestowed upon the negro as his shield and weapon for defence, the demand upon the General Government to interfere for his protection, would have been constant, irritating and embarrassing. Great complaint has been made for years past of the Government's interference, simply to secure to the colored citizen his constitutional right. But this intervention has been trifling compared to that which would have been required if we had not given suffrage to the negro." It was thus easy to infer that having instituted negro suffrage as an automatic regulator of the Southern political mechanism Northerners could turn their eyes away from what actually went on in the South. To be fair one should add that when Blaine wrote the extensive disenfranchisement of the negroes had not taken place, and that in some districts he could vote freely provided that he voted for the Democratic ticket.

It is not suggested that equal participation by the negro in Southern politics would have been automatically secured if the Radicals had succeeded in establishing the suffrage as an "inalienable right," but an unequivocal statement that all adult males had the right to vote would have been easier to enforce and more difficult to evade. Nor is it suggested that universal suffrage would have done anything to solve the vexed and unexamined question of what the negro was to do with his vote. What is suggested is that the Fifteenth Amendment was a weak compromise which failed to achieve the Radical aims and, in the long run, helped to discredit that freedom of State action which moderates wished to preserve. Under the Reconstruction Acts all "loyal" males had voted; the Fifteenth Amendment allowed States to retreat from that position while the belief that the suffrage was secured on equitable terms allowed the Northern majority to relax pressure at the point where it was most needed. The keystone of the Radical arch proved too weak to hold up the edifice. In a sense negro suffrage was premature—though it could have been written into the law at no other time—but this was only in part the result of negro immaturity. Beneath the surface of the suffrage question lay larger problems of the role of government in a democratic State and these American society as a whole was unwilling or unready to contemplate. By 1880 *The Nation*, which had earlier given somewhat lukewarm support to negro suffrage while insisting that it should be impartial and not universal, was emphasizing that the *quality* of voters should be the primary consideration. For the intelligentsia who had, for the most part, thrown their influence be-

hind Radical Republicanism, the great national problem was no longer the protection of negro rights but the defence of public morality, social respectability and economic orthodoxy against demagogues, bosses, agitators, agrarian Radicals, and mass ignorance.

It has been argued in the preceding pages that an essential weakness in the Radical programme lay in its demand for national intervention to secure equality and protect rights, exercising a power which was unfamiliar and depending upon the support of public opinion which might well be apathetic or even hostile to its objectives. The arguments for enlarged national power were made clearly and forcibly, and there was no failure on the part of the Radicals to realize that their policy demanded the use of national authority not only on a greater scale than ever before but also upon new principles. The idea which had been presented in Sumner's "Freedom National" speech of 1852 had germinated and grown until it was possible to see the nation newly based upon equal right and abandoning the divided sovreignty of the past. "It certainly seems desirable," said the moderate Luke Poland in 1866, "that no doubt should be left as to the power of Congress to enforce principles lying at the very foundation of all Republican government if they be denied or violated by the States." This was a constant theme of the Republican party and one which brought forth the most bitter cries of anguish from their opponents. "The time was," said one Democrat in 1869, "when the suggestion of grave doubts of constitutional warrant would cause the advocates of pending measures to hesitate, to reflect. . . . Innovation and reform, however specious and desirable, were rejected at once and finally unless clearly sanctioned by constitutional authority." Six years later another Democrat expressed the common view of his party when he charged that Republican interpretation of the Constitution "freed from all verbiage and ambiguity . . . amounts simply to the assertion of a supreme power in Congress over every subject that concerns the life, liberty and property of any person within the United States; in other words over everything that is the subject of the law." The detached observer may well ask what was wrong with the exercise of such power, and why the national government should not remedy the deficiencies of the States. The Radicals did not wish to scrap the Constitution, but they thought that its failure in 1861 demonstrated the need for greater flexibility in interpretation and greater concentration of power at the centre. This may appear to have been not unreasonable, but by and large the Democrats have had the best of the argument, and modern historians have echoed their criticisms though approving an extension of national authority during the New Deal which went far beyond the wildest expectations of the Radicals. It remains to ask why the concept of strong national government, which has proved so attractive to so many men in the twentieth century, did not gather the support which might have sustained it during the later nineteenth century.

Some of the explanations are obvious. The weight of tradition was against strong national government, and the word "centralism" was bogey enough to frighten large numbers of people who would not stop to ask what was being centralized, by whom, and for what purpose. Increased national authority might put power into the hands of those who were distrusted by the would-be reformers, and the professional politician might be the beneficiary from an attempt to provide the national government with a moral purpose. Roscoe Conkling had a telling point against the opponents of "centralism" when he said that "Every civilized government may protect its citizens in the uttermost ends of the earth, but when the United States interposes to check murders, and burnings, and barbarities at which humanity shudders, perpetrated by thousands, and overawing all local authority, it is suddenly discovered that we are in danger of 'centralism'." Yet for many people the argument against "centralism" was epitomized in the fear that it might increase the power of men like Roscoe Conkling; they could not ignore the fact that his vehemence against civil service reformers was as great as that against the perpetrators of Southern atrocities.

In their presentation of the case for national power the Radicals were inhibited by conventional American and nineteenth-century political thought. While the old Whigs, whose ideas they inherited, had believed in more positive action by the national government than their Democratic opponents, they had never thought of writing a blank cheque for government intervention. What they wanted was Federal responsibility for the performance of certain economic functions defined by the economic interests concerned, and since that time the concepts of *laissez-faire* had tended to narrow the sphere of action which business interests were likely to prescribe for government. Northern intellectuals who were attracted by the political aims of Reconstruction were precisely those who were equally attracted by the utopian elements in *laissez-faire*, by the theory of natural harmony, and by the faith in betterment through individual enterprise. The government was therefore being asked to "secure the blessings of liberty" at the very time when it was being asked to contract its responsibility for "promoting the general welfare," and the hope of securing civil justice for the Southern negro was not coupled with the expectation of securing social justice for the Northern farmer and worker. Thus the Radicals' concept of national power was too wide to satisfy conservative men but not wide enough to gather support from the nineteenth-century movements of protest.

Even if the concept of national power had not suffered from these inherent weaknesses it would still have had a precarious hold upon the nation. Radical Reconstruction declared certain principles of national responsibility but it did nothing to create the institutions of government which could give these principles a permanent place on the national stage. The Freedmen's Bureau was such an institution but even its friends recognized that its life must be limited. The Fourteenth Amendment left the door open for Congress to make laws which would enforce the civil rights clause, but it did not make it mandatory for Congress to do so and the assumption was that the law would be self-enforcing through the existing machinery of government and courts. The initiative remained with the traditional instruments of government—with the President, with the judges and with the States themselves—and no new instruments of government were brought into being. One can contrast this with the experience of the New Deal with its proliferation of government agencies; when enthusiasm receded the administrative achievement remained, and many Americans (ranging from highly paid government servants to the very poor) had acquired a vested interest in these new institutions. When Radical enthusiasm withered away it left behind it no such institutional bulwarks, and when the Freedmen's Bureau expired there remained no new government departments, no new government agencies, and no administrative doctrine to carry out those obligations to citizens of the United States of which so much had been heard.

*   *   *

The arguments which have been presented in the preceding pages have attempted to show why the ideology of Radical Republicanism, which appeared so powerful during the crisis of Reconstruction, failed to gather that momentum which could have carried it forward in the years which followed. It is of course exceedingly improbable that the Radicals of the Reconstruction period could have conceived their problems in any other way or that they could have gone on to produce the ideas and institutions which would have corrected the weaknesses in their edifice. Radicalism shared the weaknesses of all liberal bourgeois movements of the nineteenth century, and it would have required a far more profound revolution in thought and action to make them view their situation through the eyes of twentieth-century liberals. In their equalitarian sentiments, in their realization that individual rights might be incompatible with local self-government, and in their attitude towards national power they were prophets of the future; yet they remained children of their age and were bound by its assumptions and inhibitions. And even if their vision occasionally transcended these limitations they were unlikely to persuade the majority of their countrymen that the revolution which they had initiated ought to proceed to further innovation. The failure of Radicalism is thus a part of the wider failure of bourgeois liberalism to solve the problems of the new age which was dawning; but having said this it is important to remember that if the Radicals shared in the weaknesses of their age they also had some achievements which were exceptional.

First among civilized nations the United States had met the problems of a bi-racial society, and first among civilized nations they had committed themselves to the proposition that in such a society human beings must have equal rights. If the definition of "rights" was confused the idea that they must be recognized was clear. The civil rights clause of the Fourteenth Amendment was in many ways unsatisfactory, but it contained explosive material which could shatter the lines of racial discrimination. The United States had committed themselves to the statement that suffrage should be colour-blind, and if the phrasing of the Fifteenth Amendment invited evasion the principle which it enunciated would outlive attempts to defeat it. Americans may well differ upon the wisdom of these equalitarian ideas, but it is impossible to deny their importance for the future. The Fourteenth and Fifteenth Amendments could have been enacted only during the period of Reconstruction, and without them the subsequent history of the United States would have been very different. Not least important has been their effect upon the negro race in America, for the knowledge that the goals of negro aspiration are already written into the Constitution has had the powerful consequence of turning American negroes aside from thoughts of revolution. In his quest for equality the negro appeals to established national law and not against it, and one of the most striking developments of twentieth-century history has been the failure of Communists amongst a people who had many reasons for disaffection. The constitutional amendments had an equally powerful effect upon Northern thought. If Northern opinion, in the later years of the nineteenth century, was not prepared to implement the principles of the amendments, they were not removed from the Constitution and were to become the basis for further thought about the problem of race in America and in the world at large. It is possible to attribute the modern American hostility to "colonialism"—which so often embarrasses the European allies of the United States—to memories of the Revolution, to ingrained suspicion of Great Britain and to mere calculation about the changing balance of power in the world; but it is equally significant that during Reconstruction Americans rejected the idea that law should recognize the "inferiority" of non-European races. These are not unimportant consequences and may serve to lighten the gloom with which Americans have been accustomed to regard the crisis of Reconstruction.

When did segregation become an integral part of southern life? JOEL WILLIAMSON (b. 1930), who teaches history at the University of North Carolina, discusses this question in *After Slavery: The Negro in South Carolina During Reconstruction.* Like Brock, he sees a strong relationship between racial ideology and practice. With the abolition of slavery white southerners could no longer rely on the peculiar institution as a vehicle to enforce their racial views. Williamson analyzes the adoption of segregation practices during Reconstruction as an attempt to fill that void. His view of when and why the separation of the races became an established fact in the South should be compared to that of Woodward in the next selection.*

The Separation of the Races During Reconstruction

The physical separation of the races was the most revolutionary change in relations between whites and Negroes in South Carolina during Reconstruction.

Separation had, of course, marked the Negro in slavery; yet the very nature of slavery necessitated a constant, physical intimacy between the races. In the peculiar institution, the white man had constantly and closely to oversee the labor of the Negro, preserve order in domestic arrangements within the slave quarters, and minister to the physical, medical, and moral needs of his laborers. In brief, slavery enforced its own special brand of interracial associations; in a sense, it married the interests of white to black at birth and the union followed both to the grave. Slavery watched the great mass of Negroes in South Carolina, but those Negroes who lived outside of the slave system were not exempt from the scrutiny of the whites. Even in Charleston, the free Negro community was never large enough to establish its economic and racial independence. In the mid-nineteenth century, as the bonds of slavery tightened, the whites were forced to bring free Negroes under ever more stringent controls and to subject their lives to the closest surveillance.

During the spring and summer of

* From Joel Williamson, *After Slavery: The Negro in South Carolina During Reconstruction, 1861-1877* (Chapel Hill, N.C.: The University of North Carolina Press, 1965), pp. 274-281, 290-292, 298-299. Footnotes omitted.

1865, as the centripetal force of slavery melted rapidly away, each race clearly tended to disassociate itself from the other. The trend was evident in every phase of human endeavor: agriculture, business, occupations, schools and churches, in every aspect of social intercourse and politics. As early as July of 1865, a Bostonian in Charleston reported that "the worst sign here . . . is the growth of a bitter and hostile spirit between blacks and whites—a gap opening between the races which, it would seem may at some time result seriously." Well before the end of Reconstruction, separation had crystallized into a comprehensive pattern which, in its essence, remained unaltered until the middle of the twentieth century.

There is no clear, concise answer to the question of why separation occurred. Certainly, it was not simply a response of Negroes to the prejudiced fiat of dominant whites; nor was it a totally rationalized reaction on the part of either race. Actually, articulate whites and Negroes seldom attempted to explain their behavior. Yet, the philosophies and attitudes each race adopted toward the other lend a certain rationality to separation, and, if we are always mindful that this analysis presumes a unity which they never expressed, can be applied to promote an understanding of the phenomenon.

For the native white community, separation was a means of avoiding or minimizing problems which, they felt, would inevitably arise from the inherent inferiority of the Negro, problems which the North, in eradicating slavery and disallowing the Black Code, would not allow them to control by overt political means. In this limited sense, segregation was a substitute for slavery.

Thus, first, total separation was essential to racial purity, and racial purity was necessary to the preservation of a superior civilization which the whites had labored so arduously to construct, and suffered a long and bloody war to defend. After the war, that civilization was embattled, but not necessarily lost. Unguarded association with an inferior caste would obviously endanger white culture. In this view, children were peculiarly susceptible to damage. "Don't imagine that I allow my children to be with negroes out of my presence," wrote the mistress of a lowcountry plantation in 1868, "on one occasion only have they been so with my knowledge." Even the Negro wet nurse, that quintessence of maternalism upon which the slave period paternalist so often turned his case, emerged as the incubus of Southern infancy. "We gave our infants to the black wenches to suckle," lamented an elderly white, "and thus poisoned the blood of our children, and made them *cowards* . . . the Character of the people of the state was ruined by slavery and it will take 500 years, if not longer, by the infusion of new blood to eradicate the hereditary vices imbibed with the blood (milk is blood) of black wet nurses." Adults, of course, were not immune to racial contamination. Casual associations across the color line might lead to serious ones and to the total pollution of the superior race. Particularly might this be so of the poor, the ignorant, and the feeble-minded, but even the aristocracy had to be watched. Shortly after Redemption, an anonymous Carolinian was incensed at a rumor that Wade Hampton had dined at a table with Negroes in the home of the president of Claflin, the leading Negro university in the state. "Who shall say where it will stop?" he warned. "Will not dining lead to dancing, to social equality, to miscegenation, to mexicanization and to general damnation."

Separation also facilitated the subordination of the inferior race by constantly reminding the Negro that he lived in a world in which the white man was dominant, and in which the nonwhite was steadfastly denied access to the higher caste. Further, the impression of Negro inferiority would be constantly re-enforced by relegating the baser element, whenever possible, to the use of inferior facilities. The sheer totality of the display alone might well serve to convince members of the lower caste that such, indeed, was in the natural order of things.

Many whites had envisioned the early elimination of the freedman from the Southern scene, and many had eagerly anticipated this event. In time, however, it became evident to all that the Negro would be neither dissolved nor transported to Africa. In a sense, separation was a means of securing the quasi elimination of Negroes at home. It was, perhaps, a more satisfactory solution than their demise or emigration, since it might produce many of the benefits of their disappearance without losing an advantageous, indeed, a necessary supply of labor.

Finally, separation was a logical solution to the problem posed by the widespread conviction that the races were inherently incompatible outside of the master-slave relationship. If the white man could not exist in contentment in the proximity of Negroes, then partial satisfaction might be achieved by withdrawal from associations with members of the inferior caste. This spirit was evident among some of the wealthier whites who voluntarily dispensed entirely with the services of Negro domestics. Elderly William Heyward, in 1868 still second to none in the ranks of the rice aristocracy, stopped taking his meals at the Charleston Hotel because, as he said, he found "the negro waiters so defiant and so familiar in their attentions." "A part of the satisfaction is," he explained to a friend, "that I am perfectly independent of having negroes about me; if I cannot have them as they used to be, I have no desire to see them except in the field." Planters were often manifesting precisely the same sentiment when they deserted their land and turned to grain culture, or to the use of immigrant labor. Separation was also a way of avoiding interracial violence. B. O. Duncan and James L. Orr, both native white Republicans, argued against mixing in the public schools because they were convinced that minor irritations between children would generate major altercations between parents of different races. Conceived as a means of avoiding violence, separation, ironically, was subsequently enforced by the use of violence.

The Southern white did not always have a clear reason why racial "mixing" (as they called it) in a given situation was wrong, why the color bar should be leveled in one place and not in another. Nevertheless, he had no difficulty in recognizing a breach of the proprieties when he saw it. A young Carolinian visiting New York in the summer of 1867 was outraged by the degree of mixing he observed there: "I can now say that I have seen the city of cities, and after I have seen it it is nothing but vanity and vexation of spirit. Here you can see the negro all on equal footing with white man. White man walking the street with negroe wenches. White man and negroe riding to gether. White man and negroes sit in the same seat in church or in a word the negro enjoys the same privileges as the white man. They address each other as Mr and Miss but notwithstanding all this we (the southern boys) say what we please and when we please. . . ."

Contrary to common belief, the separation of the races was not entirely the work of the whites. Suspicious, resentful, and sometimes hateful toward the whites, chafed by white attitudes of superiority, and irritated by individual contacts with supercilious whites, Negroes, too, sought relief in withdrawal from association with the other race. In many instances, the disassociation was complete—that is, many Negroes left the state. During the war, Corporal Simon Crum of the First South Carolina declared his intention of leaving South Carolina after the capitulation because, as he phrased it, "dese yer Secesh will neber be cibilized in my time." For those who could not or would not leave, alternative forms of withdrawal were possible. A major facet in the new pattern of agriculture was the removal of Negro labor from the immediate supervision of white men. As the Negro agriculturalist moved his labor away from the eye of the white man, so also did he move his family and his home. Plantation villages became increasingly rare as Negro landowners and renters either built new houses on their plots, or, in a rather graphic symbolic display, laboriously

dragged their cabins away from the "Negro street." Negroes in the trades and in domestic service followed similar trends. Furthermore, Negroes chose to withdraw from white-dominated churches, though they were often urged to stay, and they attended racially separated schools in spite of the legal fact that all schools were open to all races. Negroes also tended to withdraw from political association with members of the white community.

Finally, on those few occasions when Negroes entered into polite social situations with whites, Northern as well as Southern, they were often ill at ease. For instance, while driving along a road near Columbia, a planter and his wife met William, "a fine looking light mulatto" who had been their stableboy as a slave. William was driving a buggy and seated beside him was a young white woman, elegantly attired. The woman was a "Yankee school marm," probably one of the new teachers in Columbia's Negro school. As he passed his late master and mistress, the Negro averted his gaze and did not speak. The following day, he approached the planter and apologized for having been escort to a "white woman." He had met the teacher at a celebration, he explained, and she had insisted on his taking her to see the countryside.

During Reconstruction, the Negro's withdrawal was never a categorical rejection of the white man and his society. In the early days of freedom, it was primarily a reaction against slavery, an attempt to escape the unpleasant associations of his previous condition and the derogatory implications of human bondage. However, as the memory of slavery faded, a more persistent reason for withdrawal emerged. Essentially, it was the

Negro's answer to discrimination. Almost invariably, attempts by individual Negroes to establish satisfactory relations across the race line were unsuccessful, and, all too often, the pain of the experience was greater than the reward for having stood for principle. During Reconstruction and afterward, only a few were willing to undergo such pain without the certainty of success. It was much easier, after all, simply to withdraw.

Withdrawal as a solution to the race problem was by no means satisfactory to the Negro leadership. Implicit in the behavior of Negro leaders during Reconstruction was a yearning for complete and unreserved acceptance for members of their race by the white community. However, overtly, and rather politically, they carefully distinguished between "social equality" and what might be appropriately termed "public equality." For themselves, they claimed only the latter. "Our race do not demand social equality," declared W. J. Whipper, a member from Beaufort, on the floor of the house of representatives in Columbia. "No law can compel me to put myself on an equality with some white men I know," he continued, and, turning cynically on a native white Republican who had vigorously defended separation, concluded, "but talk about equality and the member imagines he must take you into his arms as he probably would your sister, if she was good looking." Two years later, Martin Delany, a man who expressed pride in his blackness, said much the same thing to a large Charleston audience. "I don't believe in social equality; there is no such thing," he shouted. "If we went to associate with a man, we'll do it, and without laws."

What the Negro leadership did insist upon was public equality, that is, absolute civil and political parity with whites and full and free access to most public facilities. These latter included restaurants, bars, saloons, railway and street cars, shipboard accommodations, the theater, and other such places of public amusement. Once they gained political power, Negro leaders hastened to embody this attitude in legislation. Within a week after the first sitting of the Constitutional Convention of 1868, a Negro delegate introduced a resolution which was eventually included in the state's bill of rights: "Distinction on account of race or color, in any case whatever, shall be prohibited, and all classes of citizens shall enjoy equally all common, public, legal and political privileges." Similarly, one of the first bills passed by the Republican legislature prohibited licensed businesses from discriminating "between persons, on account of race, color, or previous condition, who shall make lawful application for the benefit of such business, calling or pursuit." Convicted violators were liable to a fine of not less than $1,000 or imprisonment for not less than a year. During the debate on the measure in the house, not a single Negro member spoke against the bill, and only five of the twenty-four votes registered against it were cast by Negroes, while fifty-three of the sixty-one votes which secured its pasage were those of Negro legislators.

Negro Congressmen were no less ardent in championing the same cause in Washington, particularly in 1874, when a federal civil rights bill was up for consideration. ". . . is it pretended anywhere," asked Congressman R. B. Elliott, who had only recently been denied service in the restaurant of a railway station in North Carolina on his journey to the capital, "that the evils of which we complain, our exclusion from the public inn, from the saloon and table of the steamboat, from the sleeping-coach on the railway, from the right of sepulture in the public burial-ground, are an exercise of the police power of the State? . . . . Are the colored people to be assimilated to an unwholesome trade or to combustible materials, to be interdicted, to be shut up within prescribed limits?" Several days later, in the same place, Congressman R. H. Cain declared, "We do not want any discrimination to be made. I do not ask any legislation for the colored people of this country that is not applied to the white people of this country. All that we seek is equal laws, equal legislation, and equal rights throughout the length and breadth of this land."

It was upon this emotional, uneven ground that an essentially new color line was drawn. It was established in a kind of racial warfare, of assaults and withdrawals, of attacks and counterattacks. Nevertheless, well before the end of Reconstruction, both forces had been fully engaged and the line was unmistakably formed.

Even before the Radicals came into power in South Carolina in 1868, native whites had already defined a color line in government-supported institutions, on common carriers, in places of public accommodation and amusement, and, of course, in private social organizations. The degree of separation in each of these areas varied. In many instances, obviously, some compromise between expense and the desire for complete separation had to be made. Usually, the compromise involved the division of available facilities in some manner. If this was thought to be inconvenient, Negroes were totally excluded. . . .

Withdrawal was also the means by which native whites combated attempts by Republican officials to end separation in institutions supported by the government. The withdrawal of native whites from the University and the State School for the Deaf and Blind at the prospect of Negro admissions are illustrations of white determination either to maintain separation or to dispense with the services afforded by related state institutions. If the Radicals had attempted to end separation in the common schools, it is virtually certain that the whites would have removed their children from these schools too. As one post-Redemption proponent of universal education argued, separation was essential to academic progress. Only by this means, he explained to Governor Hampton, could it be achieved "without any danger of social equality—*and this is the great bug bear.*" Doubtless, it was the threat of withdrawal by the whites which dissuaded the Radical leadership from further attempts to end separation in institutions over which they had, by political means, absolute control.

Whites also refused to engage in normal civic activities in which the color line was not distinctly drawn. Thus, native whites chose not to join militia companies in which Negroes participated and were reported to be extremely apprehensive of being forced to undergo the "humiliation" of joining a mixed company. Too, whites were reluctant to sit with Negroes in the jury box. An elderly Spartanburg farmer verbalized his feelings on this point in the summer of 1869: "When I go to court & see negroes on the jury & on the stand for witnesses it makes me glad that I am so near the end of my race to sit on a jury with them I dont intend to do it we have a law that exempt a man at 65 & I take the advantage of it." This kind of withdrawal often reached odd extremes. In the spring of 1870, at the peak of the Negro leadership's drive for admission to privately owned public accommodations, the white Democrats of the Charleston Fire Department refused to decorate their engines and join in the annual parade because Negro fire companies were being allowed to march in the procession.

This general withdrawal of whites from participation in civil affairs resulted in a tendency within the white community to govern itself outside of the official system. As Reconstruction progressed, this peculiar form of dyarchy approached its logical culmination. In its last days, the Tax Union came very close to the establishment of a separate government within the state when it considered collecting a ten-mil tax from its members and supervising its expenditure, thus depriving the incumbent Radicals of the staff of political life. A year later, during the period of the dual government, a similar plan was actually implemented while the Hampton regime, governed the whites and the Chamberlain government served, virtually, a Negro constituency.

Native whites also tended to withdraw from public places where the color line could not be firmly fixed and the Negro could easily assert his equality. "The whites have, to a great extent—greater than ever before—yielded the streets to the negroes," wrote a Columbian on Christmas Day, 1868. Similarly, in Charleston, in the late spring of 1866, a young aristocrat noted that the battery with its music and strollers had been yielded to the ladies and gentlemen of non-noble lineage on Saturdays, and by all whites to the Negroes on Sundays. On Saturdays, he declared, "the battery is quite full of gentlemen and ladies but it is not much patronized by the elite. . . . On Sunday afternoon the ethiops spread themselves on the Battery."

The same reaction was manifested by the whites wherever the Negro leadership succeeded by legal means in ending separation. For instance, when Negroes won admission to the street cars of Charleston, the whites simply withdrew. "On Sunday I counted five Cars successively near the Battery crowded [with] negroes, with but one white man, the Conductor," wrote a native white in May, 1867. "The ladies are practically excluded." When Academy of Music was threatened with a discrimination suit in 1870, the white community replied with a counterthreat to withdraw its patronage and thus close the theater. Adjustment which fell short of complete separation remained unsatisfactory to whites. "Even the Theatre is an uncertain pleasure," complained a Charleston lady in 1873, "no matter how attractive the program, for you know that you may have a negro next to you." Probably many of her contemporaries found the exposure too damaging and stayed home. . . .

By the end of Reconstruction, Negroes had won the legal right to enjoy, along with whites, accommodations in all public places. In reality, however, they seldom did so. On the opposite side of the racial frontier, the pattern of separation was fixed in the minds of the whites almost simultaneously with the emancipation of the Negro. By 1868, the physical color line had, for the most part, already crystallized. During the Republican regime, it was breached only in minor ways. Once the whites regained political power, there was little need to establish legally a separation which already existed in fact. Moreover, to have done so would have been contrary to federal civil rights legislation and would have given needless offense to influential elements in the North. Finally, retention of the act had a certain propaganda value for use against liberals in the North and against Republican politicians at home. Again and again, the dead letter of the law was held up as exhibit "A" in South Carolina's case that she was being fair to the Negro in the Hampton tradition. After the federal statute was vitiated in the courts, after racial liberalism had become all but extinct in the North, and as the Negro was totally disfranchised in South Carolina, the white community was ready and able to close the few gaps which did exist in the color line, and to codify a social order which custom had already decreed.

Ultimately, the physical separation of the races is the least important portion of the story. The real separation was not that duo-chromatic order that prevailed on streetcars and trains, or in restaurants, saloons, and cemeteries. The real color line lived in the minds of individuals of each race, and it had achieved full growth even before freedom for the Negro was born. Physical separation merely symbolized and reinforced mental separation. It is true that vigorous assaults by one side or the other forced the enemy to yield his forward trenches and to alter slightly the precise line of the color front. It is also true that material changes in post-Reconstruction Southern society pushed the trenches into areas which had not existed before. This often gave the illusion of basic change, of a breakthrough by the dominate whites in the war of races, whereas, actually, it merely represented the extension of the old attitudinal conflict onto new ground, only to bring with it the stalemate that marked the struggle elsewhere. Viewed in relation to the total geography of race relations, the frontier hardly changed; and the rigidity of the physical situation, set as it was like a mosaic in black and white, itself suggested the intransigence of spirit which lay behind it. Well before the end of Reconstruction, this mental pattern was fixed; the heartland of racial exclusiveness remained inviolate; and South Carolina had become, in reality, two communities—one white and the other Negro.

Sterling Professor of History at Yale University, C. VANN WOODWARD (b. 1908) has written extensively on southern history. Awarded the Bancroft Prize in 1952 for his *Origins of the New South, 1877–1913* (1951), he is also author of *The Burden of Southern History* (1960) and *Reunion and Reaction: The Compromise of 1877 and the End of Reconstruction* (1951). In the following selection, Woodward asserts that a comprehensive system of segregation entered southern life at a date later than those advanced by Williamson and the Dunningites. There is an important difference, he finds, between informal practices and an inflexible legal code. How different are the relations between the races in the period between the Compromise of 1877 and the turn of the twentieth century from those during Reconstruction and the early 1900s?*

▶ *Forgotten Alternatives*

In the South the traumatic experiences of Civil War, invasion, defeat, emancipation, occupation, and reconstruction had profound and complex—sometimes contradictory—effects on racial relations. The immediate response to the collapse of slavery was often a simultaneous withdrawal of both races from the enforced intimacy and the more burdensome obligations imposed by the old regime on each. Denied the benefits of slavery, whites shook off its responsibilities—excess hands, dependents too old or too ill or too young to work, tenants too poor to pay rent. Freedmen for their part often fled old masters and put behind them old grievances, hatreds, and the scene of old humiliations. One of the most momentous of racial separations was the voluntary withdrawal of the Negroes from the white-dominated Protestant churches, often over white protest, in order to establish and control their own separate religious institutions. In these and other ways the new order added physical distance to social distance between the races.

The separations were not all voluntary. Whites clung unwaveringly to the old doctrine of white supremacy and innate Negro inferiority that had been sustained by the old regime. It still re-

---

* From *The Strange Career of Jim Crow*, Second Revised Edition, by C. Vann Woodward. Copyright © 1966 by Oxford University Press, Inc. Reprinted by permission. Pp. 22–35.

mained to be seen what institutions or laws or customs would be necessary to maintain white control now that slavery was gone. Under slavery, control was best maintained by a large degree of physical contact and association. Under the strange new order the old methods were not always available or applicable, though the contacts and associations they produced did not all disappear at once. To the dominant whites it began to appear that the new order required a certain amount of compulsory separation of the races.

The temporary anarchy that followed the collapse of the old discipline produced a state of mind bordering on hysteria among Southern white people. The first year a great fear of black insurrection and revenge seized many minds, and for a longer time the conviction prevailed that Negroes could not be induced to work without compulsion. Large numbers of temporarily uprooted freedmen roamed the highways, congested in towns and cities, or joined the federal militia. In the presence of these conditions the provisional legislatures established by President Johnson in 1865 adopted the notorious Black Codes. Some of them were intended to establish systems of peonage or apprenticeship resembling slavery. Three states at this time adopted laws that made racial discrimination of various kinds on railroads. Mississippi gave the force of law to practices already adopted by railroads by forbidding "any freedman, negro, or mulatto to ride in any first-class passenger cars, set apart, or used by and for white persons." Nothing was said about the mixing of races in second-class cars, and no car was required for exclusive use of Negroes. The Florida

legislature went a step further the same year by forbidding whites to use cars set apart for use of Negroes, as well as excluding Negroes from cars reserved for whites, but it did not require the railroads to provide separate cars for either race, nor did it prohibit mixing of the races in smoking cars. Texas carried the development further in 1866 with a law that required all railroad companies to "attach to passenger trains one car for the special accommodation of freedmen." These three laws, as well as local ordinances of this character, were on the books only a short while, however, for they were either disallowed by military government or repealed by subsequent legislatures. Regardless of the law, the discriminatory practice of denying Negroes the use of first-class accommodations nevertheless continued on many railroads throughout Reconstruction and beyond. Not until the arrival of the full Jim Crow system much later, however, was the separation of the races required in second-class coaches or universal in first-class cars.

Other aspects of segregation appeared early and widely and were sanctioned by Reconstruction authorities. The most conspicuous of these was the segregation of the public schools. While the law might not provide for it and individuals might deplore it, segregation of the schools nevertheless took place promptly and prevailed continuously. There were very few exceptions. The only notable one was the public schools of New Orleans, which were thoroughly and successfully integrated until 1877. Attempts elsewhere were probably restrained by the knowledge that the whites would withdraw if integration were attempted. This in fact did occur at times when desegregation of colleges and other institutions was attempted. This situation prevailed generally throughout major government-supported services and facilities. The law sometimes provided for separate facilities for the races during Reconstruction. But even when this was not the case, and when both races were housed in the same jails, hospitals, or asylums, they were usually quartered in separate cells, floors, or wings. All these practices, legal or extra-legal, had the consent or at least the acquiescence of the Reconstruction governments.

In view of the degree of racial separation developed during Reconstruction, some historians have concluded that the full-blown Jim Crow system sprang up immediately after the end of slavery to take the place of the Peculiar Institution. In a full and interesting study of the Negro in South Carolina entitled *After Slavery*, Joel Williamson finds that while "slavery necessitated a constant, physical intimacy," emancipation precipitated an immediate and revolutionary separation of races. "Well before the end of Reconstruction," he writes, "separation had crystalized into a comprehensive pattern which, in its essence, remained unaltered until the middle of the twentieth century."

The experience of South Carolina may have been exceptional in some respects. But in most parts of the South, including South Carolina, race relations during Reconstruction could not be said to have crystalized or stablized nor to have become what they later became. There were too many cross currents and contradictions, revolutionary innovations and violent reactions. Racial relations of the old-regime pattern often persisted stubbornly into the new order

and met head-on with interracial encounters of an entirely new and sometimes equalitarian type. Freedman and white man might turn from a back-door encounter of the traditional sort to a strained man-to-man contact of the awkward new type within the same day. Black faces continued to appear at the back door, but they also began to appear in wholly unprecedented and unexpected places—in the jury box and on the judge's bench, in council chamber and legislative hall, at the polls and the market place. Neither of these contrasting types of contract, the old or the new, was stable or destined to endure for very long, but for a time old and new rubbed shoulders—and so did black and white—in a manner that differed significantly from Jim Crow of the future or slavery of the past.

What happened in North Carolina was a revelation to conservative whites. "It is amazing," wrote Kemp Battle of Raleigh, "how quietly our people take negro juries, or rather negroes on juries." Randolph Shotwell of Rutherfordton was dismayed on seeing "long processions of countrymen entering the village by the various roads mounted and afoot, whites and blacks marching together, and in frequent instances arm-in-arm, a sight to disguest even a decent negro." It was disturbing even to native white radicals, as one of them admitted in the Raleigh *Standard*, to find at times "the two races now eat together at the same table, sit together in the same room, work together, visit and hold debating societies together." It is not that such occurrences were typical or very common, but that they could happen at all that was important.

Southern Negroes responded to news

of the Reconstruction Act of March 1867 with numerous demonstrations against incipient Jim Crowism. In New Orleans they demonstrated so vigorously and persistently against the Jim Crow "Star Cars" established in 1864 that General Phil Sheridan ordered an end to racial discrimination on streets cars in May 1867. Similar demonstrations and what would now be called "sit-ins" brought an end about the same time to segregated street cars in Richmond, Charleston, and other cities. One of the strongest demands of the freedmen upon the new radical state legislatures of 1868 in South Carolina and Mississippi was for civil rights laws that would protect their rights on common carriers and public accommodations. The law makers of those states and others responded with comprehensive anti-discrimination statutes. Their impact was noted in South Carolina in 1868 by Elizabeth H. Botume, a Northern teacher, on a previously segregated river steamer from Charleston to Beaufort. She witnessed "a decided change" among Negro passengers, previously excluded from the upper deck. "They were everywhere," she wrote, "choosing the best staterooms and best seats at the table. Two prominent colored members of the State Legislature were on board with their families. There were also several well-known Southerners, still uncompromising rebels. It was a curious scene and full of significance." In North Carolina shortly after the adoption of the Federal Civil Rights Act of 1875 Negroes in various parts of the state successfully tested their rights in railroads, steamboats, hotels, theaters, and other public accommodations. One Negro took the railroad from Raleigh to Savannah and reported no difficulty riding and dining unsegregated. Future Congressman James E. O'Hara, a Negro, successfully integrated a steamer from Greenville to Tarboro.

As a rule, however, Negroes were not aggressive in pressing their rights, even after they were assured them by law and protected in exercising them by the federal presence. It was easier to avoid painful rebuff or insult by refraining from the test of rights. Negroes rarely intruded upon hotels or restaurants where they were unwelcome. Whites often withdrew from desegregated facilities or cut down their patronage. Negro spokesmen constantly reiterated their disavowal of aspirations for what they called "social equality," and insisted that they were concerned only for "public equality," by which they apparently meant civil and political rights. Actually there is little evidence of racial mixing on social occasions during Reconstruction, though there was much mixing on public occasions, particularly of a political character. Native white Republicans were conscious of their minority status and their desperate need for black support. As one of them wrote the Governor of Alabama, "we must have men who will mix with the negroes & tell them of their rights. If we don't have such men, we will be defeated." Such men, native white Alabamians, were found, and they worked with a will across the color line.

It would be wrong to exaggerate the amount of interracial association and intimacy produced during Reconstruction or to misconstrue its character and meaning. If the intimacy of the old regime had its unhappy and painful aspects, so did that of the new order. Unlike the quality of mercy, it was strained.

It was also temporary, and it was usually self-conscious. It was a product of contrived circumstances, and neither race had time to become fully accustomed to the change or feel natural in the relationship. Nevertheless, it would be a mistaken effort to equate this period in racial relations with either the old regime of slavery or with the future rule of Jim Crow. It was too exceptional. It is impossible to conceive of innumerable events and interracial experiments and contacts of the 1860's taking place in the 1900's. To attempt that would be to do violence to the nuances of history.

The Redeemers who overthrew Reconstruction and established "Home Rule" in the Southern states conducted their campaign in the name of white supremacy. The new rulers did not, however, inaugurate any revolution in the customs and laws governing racial relations. They retained such segregation practices as had grown up during Reconstruction, but showed no disposition to expand or universalize the system. Separation of the races continued to be the rule in churches and schools, in military life and public institutions as it had been before. And as the new governments added what few new public services they built—schools, hospitals, asylums, and the like—they applied existing practices of segregation, sometimes by law and sometimes without. But the new order represented no striking departures in this respect.

After Redemption the old and the new in race relations continued to overlap as they had during Reconstruction. The old heritage of slavery and the new and insecure heritage of legal equality were wholly incompatible as ideas, but each in its own way assured a degree of human contact and association that would pass with the fading of the old heritage and the eventual destruction of the new. Race relations after Redemption were an unstable interlude before the passing of these old and new traditions and the arrival of the Jim Crow code and disfranchisement.

One heritage of the old order that persisted far into the new was the pattern of residential mixture in the older cities and towns. A Northern reporter remarked with puzzlement in 1880 upon "the proximity and confusion, so to speak, of white and negro houses" in both the countryside and cities of South Carolina. This pattern of "proximity and confusion" continued for decades in the older parts of the South. Another heritage of the old order that kept physical contact between the races from becoming an issue and an irritant was both psychological and economic. The Negro bred to slavery was typically ignorant and poor and was not given to pressing his rights to such luxuries as hotels, restaurants, and theaters even when he could afford them or was aware of them. So far as his status was concerned, there was little need for Jim Crow laws to establish what the lingering stigma of slavery—in bearing, speech, and manner —made so apparent.

At the same time the more confident, assertive, and ambitious members of the race had not forgotten the vision of civil rights and equality that Reconstruction had inspired. Still fresh in their memories was an exhilarating if precarious taste of recognition and power. The hopes and expectations aroused by these experiences had been dimmed but not extinguished by the Compromise of 1877.

The laws were still on the books, and the whites had learned some measure of accommodation. Negroes still voted in large numbers, held numerous elective and appointive offices, and appealed to the courts with hope for redress of grievances. Under these circumstances a great deal of variety and inconsistency prevailed in race relations from state to state and within a state. It was a time of experiment, testing, and uncertainty— quite different from the time of repression and rigid uniformity that was to come toward the end of the century. Alternatives were still open and real choices had to be made.

A thorough study by Charles E. Wynes, *Race Relations in Virginia*, finds that in this state "the most distinguishing factor in the complexity of social relations between the races was that of inconsistency. From 1870 to 1900, there was no generally accepted code of racial mores." During those three decades, according to this study, "at no time was it the general demand of the white populace that the Negro be disfranchised and white supremacy be made the law of the land." Until 1900, when a law requiring the separation of the races on railroad cars was adopted by a majority of one vote, "the Negro sat where he pleased and among the white passengers on perhaps a majority of the state's railroads." There were exceptions, but "they became fewer and fewer" toward the end of the period. The same was true of the street cars. In other public accommodations and places of entertainment the black patron often met with rebuff and sometimes eviction, but not always, for "occasionally the Negro met no segregation when he entered restaurants, bars, waiting rooms, theatres, and other pub-

lic places of amusement." There were risks, but no firm policy of exclusion, and this "led many Negroes to keep trying for acceptance, just as it led at least some whites to accept them." There were crosscurrents and uncertainties on both sides, but in spite of this there remained a considerable range of flexibility and tolerance in relations between the races in Virginia between 1870 and 1900.

More than a decade was to pass after Redemption before the first Jim Crow law was to appear upon the law books of a Southern state, and more than two decades before the older states of the seaboard were to adopt such laws. There was much segregation and discrimination of an extra-legal sort before the laws were adopted in all the states, but the amount of it differed from one place to another and one time to another, just as it did in Virginia.

The individual experiences and the testimony regarding them presented below are not offered as conclusive evidence or as proof of a prevailing pattern. They are the observations of intelligent men with contrasting backgrounds and origins about a fluid, continually changing, and controversial situation. It would be perfectly possible to cite contemporary experiences and testimony of a contrasting character. To appreciate the significance of the following episodes and experiences one has only to attempt to imagine any of them occurring in any of the states concerned at any time during the first half of the twentieth century. The contrast will be less immediately apparent, and perhaps even lost, to those whose personal experience and memory does not extend back quite so remotely as the 1940's, but they might ask confirmation from their elders.

Suggestions for Further Reading

Historians have produced a host of studies pertaining to the Reconstruction era. Since this bibliography can only deal with a portion of the literature, the student interested in pursuing the subject further will find the following bibliographical essays highly useful: Don E. Fehrenbacher, "Division and Reunion," in John Higham (ed.), *The Reconstruction of American History* (New York, 1962), pp. 98–118; Bernard Weisberger, "The Dark and Bloody Ground of Reconstruction Historiography," *Journal of Southern History*, XXV (November, 1959), 427–447; Vernon L. Wharton, "Reconstruction," in Arthur S. Link and Rembert W. Patrick (eds.), *Writing Southern History: Essays in Historiography in Honor of Fletcher M. Green* (Baton Rouge, 1965), pp. 295–315; and T. Harry Williams, "An Analysis of Some Reconstruction Attitudes," *Journal of Southern History*, XII (November, 1946), 469–486. For a general survey of the period, see James G. Randall and David Donald, *The Civil War and Reconstruction* (Boston, 1961), and Rembert Patrick, *The Reconstruction of the Nation* (New York, 1967).

A good introduction to the historical debate over Andrew Johnson's role in Reconstruction is Albert Castel, "Andrew Johnson: His Historiographical Rise and Fall," *Mid-America*, XLV (July, 1963), 79–98. A contemporary of James Ford Rhodes, John W. Burgess, in *Reconstruction and the Constitution, 1866–1876* (New York, 1902), supports his critical view of Johnson and the Radicals. For a view that stresses the vindictive and self-seeking characteristics of a Radical leader, see Richard N. Current, *Old Thad Stevens: A Story of Ambition* (Madison, 1942). On the other side of the controversy, there are a large number of biographical studies that defend Johnson. Among these are: George F. Milton, *The Age of Hate: Andrew Johnson and the Radicals* (New York, 1930); Lloyd P. Stryker, *Andrew Johnson: A Study of Courage* (New York, 1929); and Robert W. Winston, *Andrew Johnson: Plebian and Patriot* (New York, 1928).

Numerous studies support an economic interpretation of the presidential-congressional conflict. These include Charles and Mary Beard, *The Rise of American Civilization* (2 vols.; New York, 1927); William B. Hesseltine, "Economic Factors in the Abandonment of Reconstruction," *Mississippi Valley Historical Review*, XXII (September, 1935), 191–210; Matthew Josephson, *The Politicos* (New York, 1938); T. Harry and Helen Williams, "Wisconsin Republicans and Reconstruction, 1865–1870," *Wisconsin Magazine of History*, XXIII (September, 1939), 17–39; and George R. Woolfolk, *The Cotton Regency: The Northern Merchants and Reconstruction, 1865–1880* (New York, 1958). Critiques of the economic thesis are set forth in Robert P. Sharkey, *Money Class and Party: An Economic Study of the Civil War and Reconstruction* (Baltimore, 1959) and Irwin Unger, "Business Men and Specie Resumption," *Political Science Quarterly*, LXXIV (March, 1959), 67–90.

Many recent studies have emphasized the

division within Republican ranks and the idealism of the Radicals. An outsanding example of this viewpoint is W. R. Brock, *An American Crisis: Congress and Reconstruction, 1865-1867* (New York, 1963). Fawn M. Brodie, *Thaddeus Stevens: Scourge of the South* (New York, 1959) depicts Stevens as committed to the cause of equal rights for Negroes and disputes the contention that his control of the House was absolute. Also important for their emphasis on Radical idealism are: Irving H. Bartlett, *Wendell Phillips: Brahmin Radical* (Boston, 1962); Benjamin P. Thomas and Harold M. Hyman, *Stanton: The Life and Times of Lincoln's Secretary of War* (New York, 1962); and Hans L. Trefouse, *Benjamin F. Wade, Radical Republican from Ohio* (New York, 1963). For two examples of the quantitative approach to the problem of Radical motivation, see David Donald, *The Politics of Reconstruction, 1863-1867* (Baton Rouge, 1965) and Glenn Linden, " 'Radicals' and Economic Policies: The Senate, 1861-1873," *Journal of Southern History*, XXXII (May, 1966), 189-199.

Studies of abolitionist and Radical activity in behalf of Negro rights in the North should also be consulted. These include Ira V. Brown, "Pennsylvania and the Rights of the Negro, 1865-1887," *Pennsylvania History*, *XXVIII* (January, 1961), 45-57; David Montgomery, "Radical Republicans in Pennsylvania, 1866-1873," *Pennsylvania Magazine of History and Biography*, LXXXV (October, 1961), 439-457; and James M. McPherson's penetrating *Struggle for Equality* (Princeton, N.J., 1964). William Gillette in *The Right to Vote: Politics and the Passage of the Fifteenth Amendment* (Baltimore, Md., 1965) maintains that the primary purpose of the Amendment was to enfranchise the northern Negro.

The Dunning school has produced many studies of Congressional Reconstruction. Space allows mention of only a few of these works. Further insight into Dunning's views can be gained from his *Essays on the Civil War and Reconstruction* (New York, 1898) and the essay of Alan D. Harper, "William A. Dunning: The Historian as Nemesis," *Civil War History*, X (March, 1964), 54-66. Two volumes by Walter L. Fleming are influential but vitriolic statements of the Dunning thesis: *Civil War and Reconstruction in Alabama* (New York, 1905) and *The Sequel of Appomattox* (New Haven, Conn., 1921). For a more balanced Dunningite presentation, see C. Mildred Thompson, *Reconstruction in Georgia, Economic, Social, Political, 1865-1872* (New York, 1915). A less scholarly presentation, but one that gained wide public acceptance is Claude Bowers, *The Tragic Era: The Revolution after Lincoln* (New York, 1929). More recent examples of the Dunning thesis include E. Merton Coulter's volume in "A History of the South" series, *The South During Reconstruction, 1865-1877* (Baton Rouge, 1947); A. B. Moore's essay, "One Hundred Years of Reconstruction in the South," *Journal of Southern History*, IX (May, 1943), 153-180; and W. C. Nunn, *Texas under the Carpetbaggers* (Austin, 1962).

The literature critical of the Dunning school is extensive. Early pleas for re-examinations of the Dunningites' conclusions as well as incisive summaries of revisionist writings are contained in Howard K. Beale, "On Rewriting Reconstruction History," *American Historical Review*, XLV (July, 1940), 807-827, and Francis B. Simkins, "New Viewpoints of Southern Reconstruction," *Journal of Southern History*, V (February, 1939), 49-61. Of the early studies, the following are still valuable: Horace Mann Bond, "Social and Economic Forces in Alabama Reconstruction," *Journal of Negro History*, XXIII (July, 1938), 290-348; Francis B. Simkins and Robert H. Woody, *South Carolina During Reconstruction* (Chapel Hill, N.C., 1947); and Vernon L. Wharton's outstanding monograph, *The Negro in Mississippi, 1865-1890* (Chapel Hill, N.C., 1947). Two of the earliest revisionists viewed Reconstruction from a Marxist perspective: W. E. B. Du Bois, *Black Reconstruction in America* (New York, 1935), and James Allen, *Reconstruction: The Battle for Democracy, 1865–1867* (New York, 1937).

Since Beale's call for a re-evaluation of the Dunning school's findings, revisionist historians have published studies on almost every aspect of Reconstruction. Carl N. Degler has synthesized many revisionist conclusions in his *Out of Our Past: The Forces that Shaped Modern America* (New York, 1959), 209–228. State studies of particular significance are: Thomas B. Alexander, *Political Reconstruction in Tennessee* (Nashville, 1950); Joe M. Richardson, *The Negro in the Reconstruction of Florida, 1865–1877* (Tallahassee, Fla., 1965); and Joel Williamson, *After Slavery: The Negro in South Carolina During Reconstruction, 1861–1877* (Chapel Hill, N.C., 1965).

David Donald, "The Scalawag in Mississippi Reconstruction," *Journal of Southern History*, X (November, 1944), 447–460, disputes the simplistic characterization of the scalawags. For a similar approach to other states, see the following articles by Thomas B. Alexander: "Persistent Whiggery in Alabama and the Lower South, 1860–1877," *Alabama Review*, XII (January, 1959), 35–52; "Whiggery and Reconstruction in Tennessee," *Journal of Southern History*, XVI (August, 1950), 291–305; and "Persistent Whiggery in the Confederate South, 1860–1877," *Journal of Southern History*, XXVII (August, 1961), 305–329. There are a number of re-evaluations of the motives, composition, and accomplishments of the carpetbaggers. Among the most important are: Richard N. Current, "Carpetbaggers Reconsidered," in *A Festschrift for Frederick B. Artz* (Durham, N.C., 1964), 139–157, and Jack B. Scroggs, "Southern Reconstruction: A Radical View," *Journal of Southern History*, XXIV (November, 1958), 407–429. Also highly recommended is Otto H. Olsen's biography of a leading carpetbagger: *Carpet-*

bagger's Crusade: The Life of Albion Winegar Tourgée (Baltimore, Md., 1965).

Still to be fully explored is the Negro's role in Reconstruction. On this point, see the suggestive essays by John Hope Franklin and August Meier in Harold Hyman (ed.), *New Frontiers of the American Reconstruction* (Urbana, Ill., 1966), 59–86. Henderson Donald in *The Negro Freedmen* (New York, 1952) has attempted a comprehensive treatment of the Negro during Reconstruction. More specialized and highly illuminating are: Otis Singletary, *The Negro Militia and Reconstruction* (Austin, 1957); the works of Richardson, *Negro in . . . Florida*; Williamson, *After Slavery*; and Wharton, *Negro in Mississippi* cited earlier. The following works are still worth consulting: Luther Jackson, *Negro Office-Holders in Virginia, 1865–1895* (Norfolk, Va., 1945); and three works of A. A. Taylor: *The Negro in South Carolina During the Reconstruction* (Washington, 1924); *The Negro in Tennessee, 1865–1880* (Washington, 1941); and *The Negro in the Reconstruction of Virginia* (Washington, 1926).

The revisionists have also questioned the conclusions of the Dunning school regarding one of its leading targets—the Freedmen's Bureau. John and LaWanda Cox in "General O. O. Howard and the 'Misrepresented Bureau,'" *Journal of Southern History*, XIX (November, 1953), 427–456, have found many positive aspects in the Bureau's program and actions. Insight into the actions of the Bureau and the movement to provide land for the freedmen can be gained from Martin Abbott, "Free Land, Free Labor, and the Freedmen's Bureau," *Agricultural History*, XXX (April, 1956), 150–157; LaWanda Cox, "The Promise of Land for the Freedmen," *Mississippi Valley Historical Review*, XLV (December, 1958), 414–440; and John G. Sproat, "Blueprint for Radical Reconstruction," *Journal of Southern History*, XXIII (February, 1957), 25–44. Willie Lee Rose describes a short-lived experiment to assist the freedmen in

Rehearsal for Reconstruction: The Port Royal Experiment (Indianapolis, 1964).

The student interested in constitutional history will find an abundance of material. Good starting points are Joseph B. James, *The Framing of the Fourteenth Amendment* (Urbana, Ill., 1956); Alfred H. Kelly, "The Congressional Controversy over School Segregation, 1867–1875," *American Historical Review*, LXIV (April, 1959), 537–563; and Everette Swinney, "Enforcing the Fifteenth Amendment, 1870–1877," *Journal of Southern History*, XXVIII (May, 1962), 202–218.

In recent years historians have displayed increasing interest in both the reasons for the end of Reconstruction and the period following Redemption. A number of historians date Radical and abolitionist desertion of the freedmen from the early 1870s. See, for example, Richard Drake, "Freedmen's Aid Societies and Sectional Compromise," *Journal of Southern History*, XXIX (May, 1963), 175–186; William B. Hesseltine, "Economic Factors in the Abandonment of Reconstruction," *Mississippi Valley Historical Review*, XXII (September, 1935), 191–210; and Patrick W. Riddleberger, "The Radicals Abandonment of the Negro during Reconstruction," *Journal of Negro History*, XLV (April, 1960), 88–102. James M. McPherson, however, in "Grant or Greeley? The Abolitionist Dilemma in the Election of 1872," *American Historical Review*, LXXI (October, 1965), 43–61, asserts that a majority of the abolitionists continued to work for the enforcement of civil rights laws during the 1870s. Two studies of the Republican party challenge the assertion that Republicans lost interest in the South following the Compromise of 1877: Vincent P. De Santis, *Republicans Face the Southern Question: The New Departure Years, 1877–1897* (Baltimore, Md., 1959) and Stanley P. Hirshon, *Farewell to the Bloody Shirt: Northern Republicans and the Southern Negro, 1877–1893* (Bloomington, Ind., 1962).

The works of C. Vann Woodward are essential for an understanding of the Redeemer period. Among these, see *Reunion and Reaction: The Compromise of 1877 and the End of Reconstruction* (Boston, 1951) and *The Origins of the New South, 1877–1913* (Baton Rouge, 1951). For a comprehensive introduction to the historiography of this period, see Paul M. Gaston's "The 'New South,'" in Link and Patrick, *Writing Southern History* (Baton Rouge, 1965), 316–336. Woodward's thesis on the rise of Jim Crow is seconded by Frenise A. Logan, *The Negro in North Carolina, 1876–1894* (Chapel Hill, N.C., 1964) and Charles E. Wynes, *Race Relations in Virginia, 1870–1902* (Charlottesville, Va., 1961). Evidence of segregation practices in ante-bellum southern cities can be found in Richard C. Wade, *Slavery in the Cities: The South, 1820–1860* (New York, 1964).

As with the Reconstruction era, there is a need for more studies of the Negro in the Redeemer period. A few works now available are: Rayford W. Logan's examination of *The Negro in American Life and Thought: The Nadir, 1877–1901* (New York, 1954); the early chapters of August Meier, *Negro Thought in America, 1880–1915: Radical Ideologies in the Age of Booker T. Washington* (Ann Arbor, 1963); George B. Tindall, *South Carolina Negroes, 1877–1900* (Columbia, S.C., 1952); and the works of Logan and Wynes cited in the preceding paragraph.